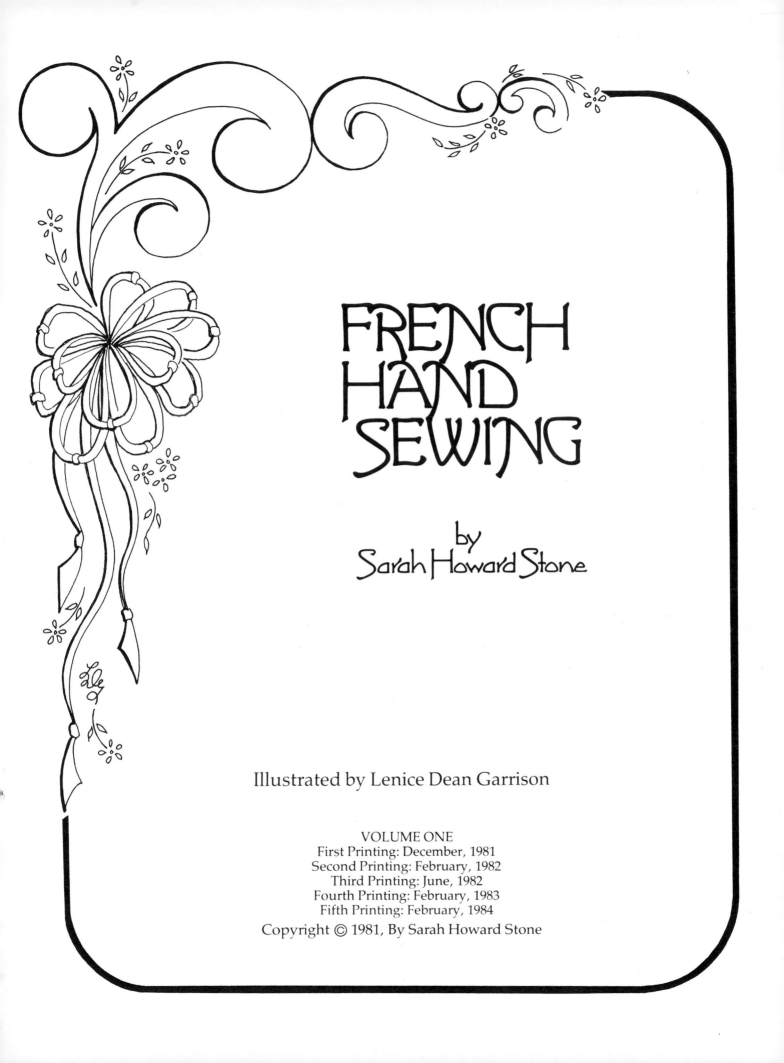

FRENCH HAND SEWING

by
Sarah Howard Stone

Illustrated by Lenice Dean Garrison

VOLUME ONE
First Printing: December, 1981
Second Printing: February, 1982
Third Printing: June, 1982
Fourth Printing: February, 1983
Fifth Printing: February, 1984

This book is dedicated to the two women who have been the greatest influence in my life:

My mother, Sara Roe Howard, who shared her many talents so generously with others and

Mary Oliver McLemore, whose quiet and gentle ways touched all who knew her.

CONTENTS

INTRODUCTION

Our ties to the past are precious. One of the gentle, sweet joys of yesteryear is French handsewing. Amazingly, the art of creating exquisite, handsewn clothes has never found its way into formalized written instruction. The art has survived since the days when nuns made clothes for royalty, and has been kept alive by means of personal instruction, from woman to woman.

The clothes which most characterize the mood achieved with French handsewing are those dating from the early 1800's to the early 1900's. It was during this period that embroidery, tucks, and puffing were used for adorning elaborate clothes and undergarments of women and children. Children's fashions had already become less constricting and this "new freedom" eventually found its way into dress for women.

Even today, only the finest materials such as batiste, lawn, and organdy are used in these handmade creations.

Extra fine thread and tiny needles are used when creating the delicate things that can be made by this art. Flowing, elaborate christening gowns and baby dresses, little boys' button-on suits, little girls' party dresses, blouses and dresses for ladies, and boudoir pillows are all made using the same basic techniques. French lace insertion and edging are used for the finishing touches.

Today, the mention of French handsewing brings to mind a picture of a little girl in a beautiful, white batiste party dress replete with lace, ruffles, and ribbons. Framing her angelic face is an absolutely splendid French Bonnet. The effect is one of softness and sweetness reminiscent of gentler times.

TERMS & DEFINITIONS

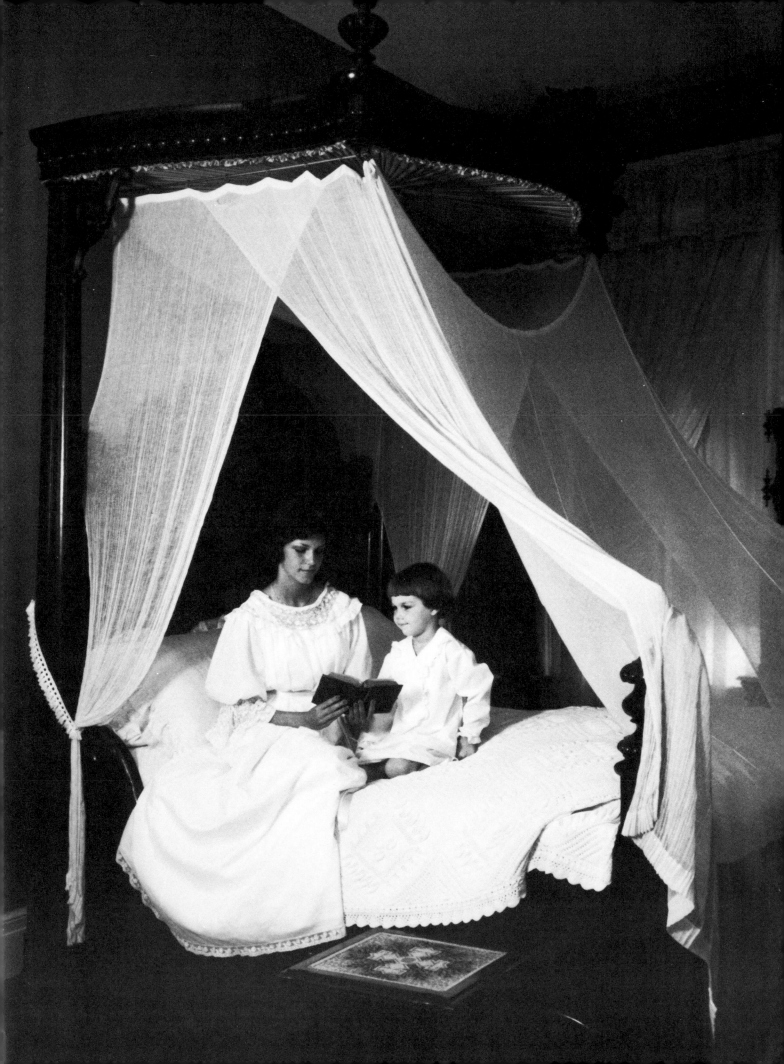

TERMS

length — warp yarns or yarns that run parallel to the selvage

width — the measurement of the yarns running from selvage to selvage

selvage — the edge of a fabric woven so that it will not ravel

bias — a line running diagonally across the grain of the fabric

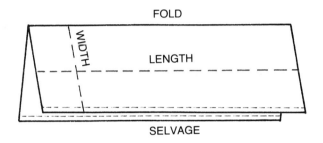

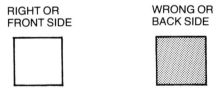

RIGHT OR FRONT SIDE   WRONG OR BACK SIDE

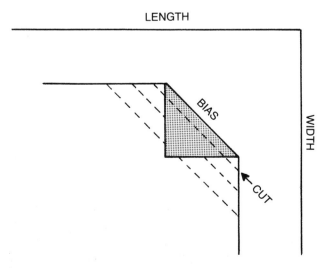

DEFINITIONS

beading edges — lace insertion with holes for ribbon to run through; can be drawn for a ruffled effect or to serve as added adornment.

beading galoon — a band with scalloped edges on both sides in a variety of widths, with holes for ribbon to run through; used for shoulder straps on camisoles, lingerie, and also for adorning dresses.

beading insertions — lace or embroidery having a straight edge on both sides with slits in the center to run ribbon through; used for baby garments, children's wear, underwear, and lingerie.

edges & flounces — lace or embroidery, with one straight side and one scalloped side; can be from 1/2 inch to 36 inches wide.

galoons — lace or embroidery with scalloped edges on both sides; can range from 1/2 inch in width to 10 inches in width.

medallions — distinct designs, pre-made or cut from lace; the light types are set in by hand on lingerie, infant wear, children's and women's garments.

insertions — lace or embroidery made with both sides straight and reinforced with extra threads or veining for added strength; used for joining pieces of fabric or trim together.

veinings — also called entredeux; used to join various parts of materials; serves both utility and ornamental purposes; can vary in width from 1/8th inch to 1/2 inch.

vraie — French word to designate a lace as "real" or handmade/

VEINING OR
ENTREDEUX

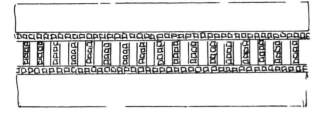

ENTREDEUX BEADING

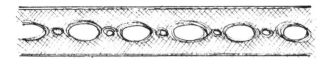

LACE BEADING

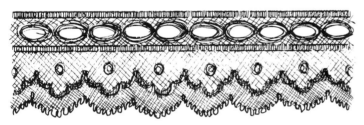

LACE BEADED EDGING

LACE INSERTION

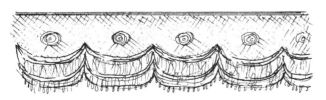

LACE FLOUNCE OR EDGING

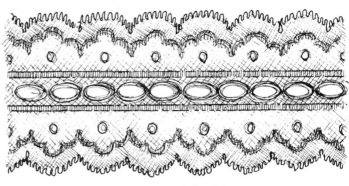

LACE BEADING GALOON

EYELET BEADING

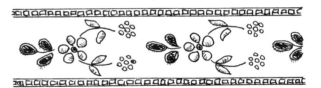

EYELET INSERTION

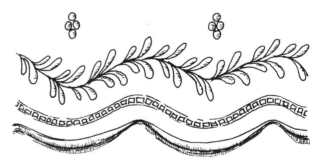

EYELET EDGING

EYELET GALOON

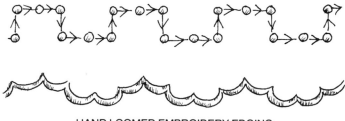

HAND LOOMED EMBROIDERY INSERTION

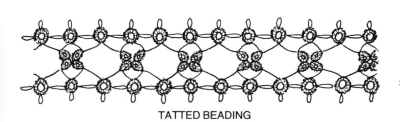

HAND LOOMED EMBROIDERY EDGING

TATTED BEADING

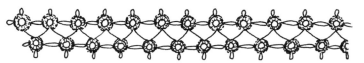

TATTED MEDALLION

TATTED INSERTION

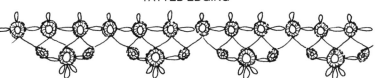

TATTED EDGING

DOUBLE TATTED EDGING

HAND LOOMED
EMBROIDERY

ENTREDEUX
LACE BEADING
ENTREDEUX
HAND LOOMED EMBROIDERY
ENTREDEUX
LACE BEADING
ENTREDEUX

ENTREDEUX
LACE INSERT
LACE BEAD
ENTREDEUX
EYELET INS.
ENT.
LACE BEAD
LACE INS.
ENT.
EYELET EDGING

ENTREDEUX
LACE INSERTION
ENTREDEUX

ENTREDEUX
LACE INSERTION
LACE INSERTION
LACE INSERTION
ENTREDEUX
HANDLOOMED EMBROIDERY
ENTREDEUX
LACE INSERTION
LACE INSERTION
LACE INSERTION
ENTREDEUX

ENTREDEUX
LACE INSERTION
ENTREDEUX

CHARTS AND MEASUREMENTS FOR GIRLS DRESSES

CHART FOR DRESS WITH PLAIN SKIRT

Age 6 mos.-2 yrs.	2 strips length needed x 33½"
Age 3-4 yrs.	2 strips length needed x 33½"
Age 5-6 yrs.	2 strips length needed x 36"
Age 7-12 yrs.	2 strips length needed x 44"

Allow 5½" to length for hem size 6 mos. to 2 yrs.
Allow 6½" to length for hem all other sizes.

CHART FOR SLEEVE RUFFLES

Age 6 mos.-2 yrs.	2 strips 1¼" x 18"
Age 3-4 yrs.	2 strips 1½" x 20"
Age 5-6 yrs.	2 strips 1¾" x 22"
Age 7-12 yrs.	2 strips 2" x 24"

Each strip makes **one** ruffle.

CHART FOR FANCY BANDS

Age 6 mos.-2 yrs.	width desired x 66½" long
Age 3 yrs.-4 yrs.	width desired x 72½" long
Age 5 yrs.-6 yrs.	width desired x 80½" long
Age 7 yrs.-12 yrs.	width desired x 87" long

CHART FOR HEM BELOW A FANCY BAND

Age 6 mos.-2 yrs.
2 strips 11" down selvage x 33½" across width
Age 3 yrs.-4 yrs.
2 strips 12" down the selvage x 36½" across width
Age 5 yrs.-6 yrs.
2 strips 12½" down selvage x 40½" across width
Age 7 yrs.-12 yrs.
2 strips 13" down selvage x 43¾" across width

CHART FOR RUFFLES FOR DRESS AND SLIP SKIRTS

Age 6 mos.-2 yrs.	3 strips 1¾" x 36" across
Age 3-4 yrs.	3 strips 2" x 36" across
Age 5-6 yrs.	3 strips 3½" x 44" across
Age 7-12 yrs.	3 strips 3½" x 44" across

CHART FOR SKIRT WITH FANCY BAND AND RUFFLE

6 mos.-2 yrs.	2 strips length needed to complete skirt x 33½"
3-4 yrs.	2 strips length needed to complete skirt x 36½"
5-6 yrs.	2 strips length needed to complete skirt x 40½"
7-12 yrs.	2 strips length needed to complete skirt x 43¾"

WIDE ENTREDEUX
LACE INSERTION
ENTREDEUX
EYELET INSERTION
ENTREDEUX
LACE INSERTION
WIDE ENT.
EYELET EDGING

LACE INSERTION
LACE BEADING
LACE INSERTION
LACE BEADING
LACE INSERTION
ENTREPEUX
LACE EDGING

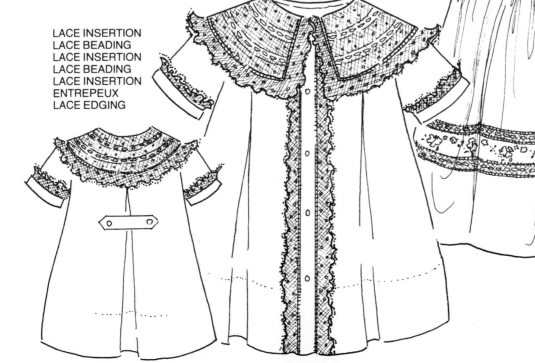

ENTREDEUX
LACE BEADING
ENTREDEUX
HAND LOOMED EMBROIDERY
ENTREDEUX
LACE BEADING
ENTREDEUX

HEAD MEASUREMENTS FOR
CAPS AND BONNETS

DISTANCE
BETWEEN
THE
FRONT
OF
BONNET
OR
CAP
TO
NAPE
OF
NECK

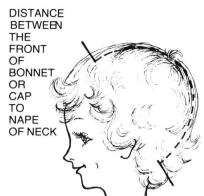

NAPE OF NECK

FROM UNDER EAR ACROSS
HEAD TO UNDER EAR

IT IS GENERALLY RECOMMENDED THAT YOU
USE A PATTERN ONE SIZE SMALLER
THAN YOUR CHILD WEARS IN A READY MADE DRESS

BACK
YOKE

LENGTH
FROM CENTER BACK NECKLINE TO FINISHED LENGTH

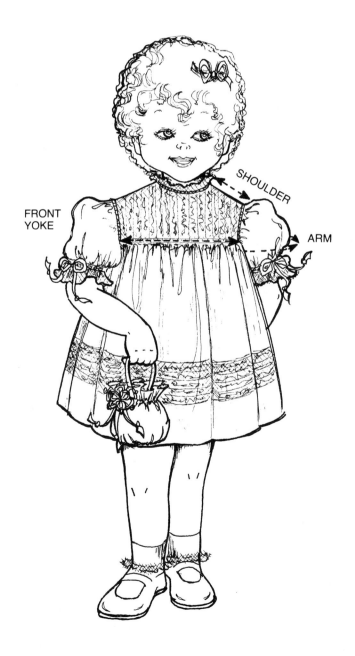

FRONT
YOKE

SHOULDER

ARM

CHARTS AND MEASUREMENTS
FOR BOYS SUITS

Boys Length from center back necklines to center of crotch

#6 mos.	— 15½″
#1	— 17½″
#2	— 18″
#3	— 19″
#4	— 20″
#5	— 21″

Chest Measurement for boys

#6 mos.	— 19″
#1	— 20″
#2	— 21″
#3	— 22″
#4	— 23″
#5	— 24″

Cuff Measurements

#6 mos.-2	— 8″
#3-5	— 9″

Measurement for sewing on shirt buttons
(underarm seam to waist)

#6 mos.	— 3″
#1	— 3½″
#2	— 4″
#3	— 4½″
#4	— 5″
#5	— 5½″

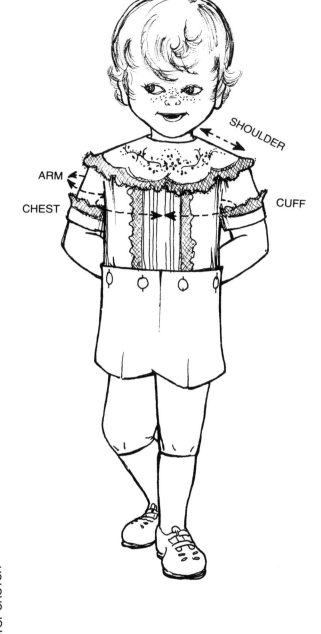

SHOULDER

ARM

CHEST

CUFF

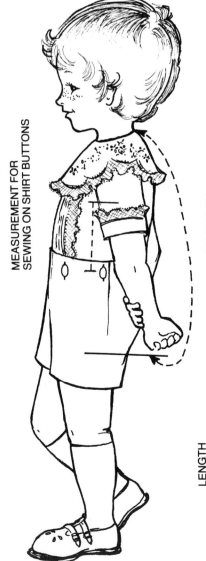

MEASUREMENT FOR
SEWING ON SHIRT BUTTONS

LENGTH
FROM CENTER BACK NECKLINE TO CENTER OF CROTCH

BASIC INSTRUCTIONS

EVEN MATERIAL

One of the most important factors in hand-sewing is to use straight strips of material.

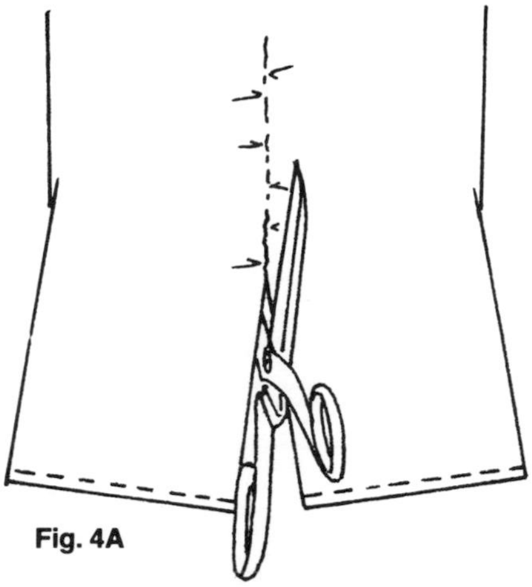

Make a clip through the selvage edge of the material. (See Figure 1A)

Pick up a horizontal thread. (See Figure 2A)

Pull the thread carefully until the desired length is reached. (See Figure 3A)

Cut the material on the pulled thread line. (See Figure 4A)

NOTE: If the thread should break before the desired length is reached, cut on the line to where line stops and pick up the thread again.

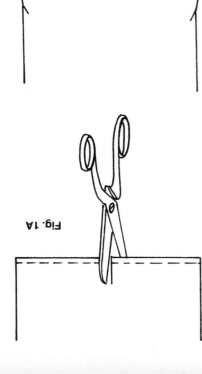

Fig. 1A

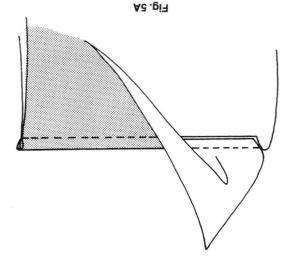

Fig. 2A

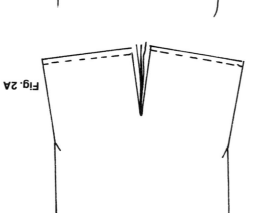

Fig. 3A

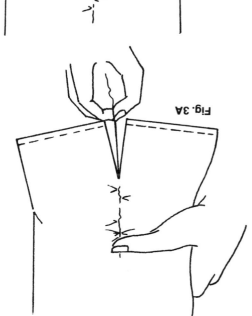

Fig. 4A

FRENCH SEAMS

Put the wrong sides of the material together and sew with tiny running stitches 1/8 inch from the raw edge.

Turn on the stitching line and press or crease with finger so the right sides of the material will be together and sew with tiny running stitches enclosing the first seam with the second seam. (See Figure 5A)

All seams should be pressed to the back of the garment.

Fig. 5A

ROLL AND WHIP

This is the most IMPORTANT STITCH IN HANDSEWING. It requires much practice to master, but it is time well spent.

Hold the top right edge of the material between the thumb and fingers, as shown in Figure 6A.

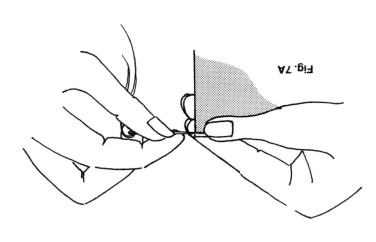

Fig. 6A

Lay the needle in a horizontal position at the top right hand corner of the material and, with the left hand, firmly roll the fabric at the same time 1/4 inch or one complete roll. (Figures 7A and 8A.)

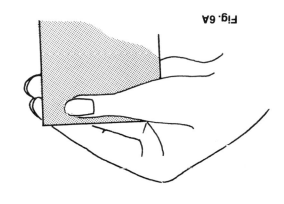

Fig. 7A

Pull the needle out of the roll and, using the right hand, slide the needle under the roll and out the top, encasing the roll but not going through the back of the material. Make the stitches 1/8 inch apart, keeping the needle at a 45 degree angle. (Figure 9A.)

Sew toward the thumb and repeat the process illustrated in Figure 8A. Occasionally, you may need to use the needle again to roll the seams and bias edges. Moisten finger if necessary to make the material roll easier.

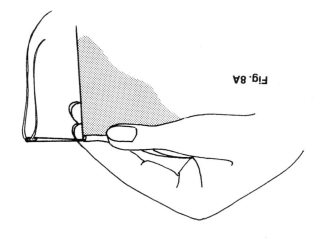

Fig. 8A

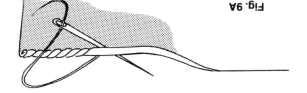

Fig. 9A

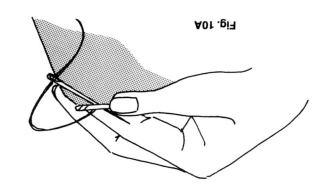

Fig. 10A

NOTE: While sewing, you may hold the material around your finger, as in Figure 10A, or you may hold the material out straight by securing the end as shown in Figure 11A.

You should be able to gather the material evenly by pulling the thread as you roll and whip. (Every two (2) to three (3) inches.) (See Figure 12A.)

NOTE: If the thread will not pull, two things may be wrong:

(a) You may have inserted your needle through the back of the material rather than through the top of the roll, or

(b) You may have let the thread get in front of the needle, therefore making a knot.

When you have mastered this stitch and are sure the rolling and whipping will gather, you may roll and whip equal sections of puffing on both sides or equal sections of ruffles on one side before pulling the thread.

Secure the end of the rolling and whipping with a slip knot. (See instructions for ending a thread.)

Starting a thread on a rolled edge without a knot

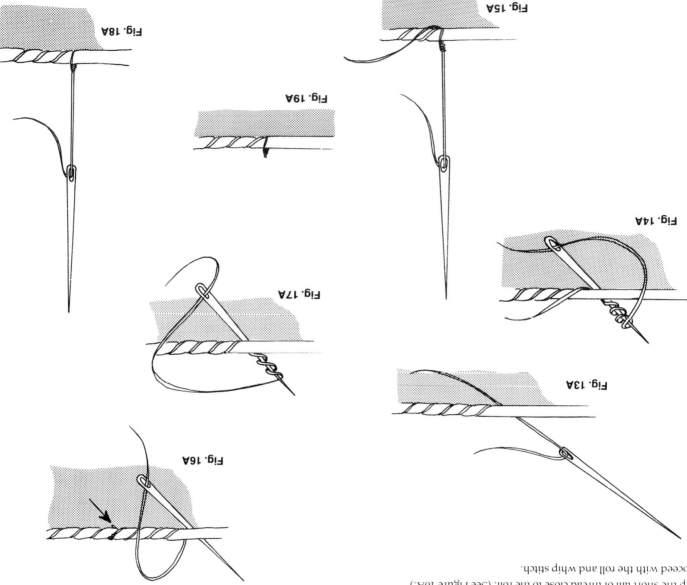

Fig. 15A

Fig. 14A

Fig. 13A

Insert the needle under the roll. Bring the needle and thread out through the top of the roll leaving a short tail of thread. (See Figure 13A.)

Hold the tail of the thread and insert the needle once again under the roll (do not pull needle out) and wrap the single thread three or four times clockwise around the needle. (See Figure 14A.)

Gently hold the wraps with the left thumb and pull the needle through the twist of thread until it forms a tight knot. (See Figure 15A.)

Clip the short tail of thread close to the roll. (See Figure 16A.)

Proceed with the roll and whip stitch.

Ending a thread on a rolled edge without a knot

Fig. 18A

Fig. 19A

Fig. 17A

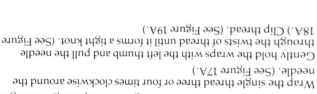

Fig. 16A

Insert the needle under the rolled edge without pulling it through.

Wrap the single thread three or four times clockwise around the needle. (See Figure 17A.)

Gently hold the wraps with the left thumb and pull the needle through the twists of thread until it forms a tight knot. (See Figure 18A.)

Clip thread. (See Figure 19A.)

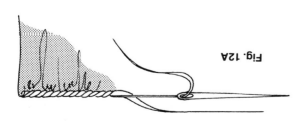

Fig. 12A

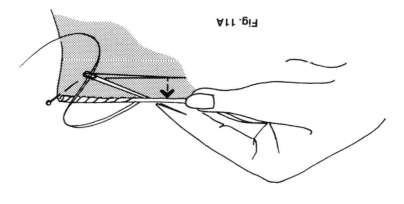

Fig. 11A

ENTREDEUX

Entredeux (or Veining) is a French word meaning "between two." The right side is raised and shiny and the wrong side is dull and flat. Trim only one (1) side at a time, as shown in Figure 20A.

APPLICATION OF ENTREDEUX TO A ROLLED EDGE

Lay the right side of the entredeux (trimmed side) to the right side of the rolled edge with the top edges even and, whipping over and over, go under the roll and through each entredeux hole. Press entredeux back and trim the other side. (See Figure 21A.)

NOTE: The roll and stitches will show if the needle is not under the roll.

APPLICATION TO A ROLLED EDGE SIDE BY SIDE

Lay the trimmed side of the entredeux next to the rolled edge of the material (side by side) with the wrong side facing you and whip together by placing the needle under the roll and through each entredeux hole. (See Figure 22A.) Trim other side of entredeux.

APPLICATION TO LACE

Lay the right side of the entredeux to the right side of the lace with the top edges even and, whipping over and over, go under the heavy lace line and through each entredeux hole. (See Figure 23A.) Press entredeux back and trim the other side.

APPLICATION TO LACE SIDE BY SIDE

Lay the trimmed side of the entredeux next to the straight edge of the lace and whip together (side by side) by taking up the heavy line on the lace and going into every entredeux hole. (See Figure 24A.) Trim other side.

APPLICATION TO LACE SCALLOP OR A CIRCLE.

Pin the lace scallop or curved edge to paper with the right side down on the paper.

Trim one (1) side of the entredeux and clip the fabric on the other side so that it will turn easily.

Pin the trimmed side next to the scalloped or curved edge, making sure that it is full enough so that it will not pucker; whip together side by side. (See Figure 25A.)

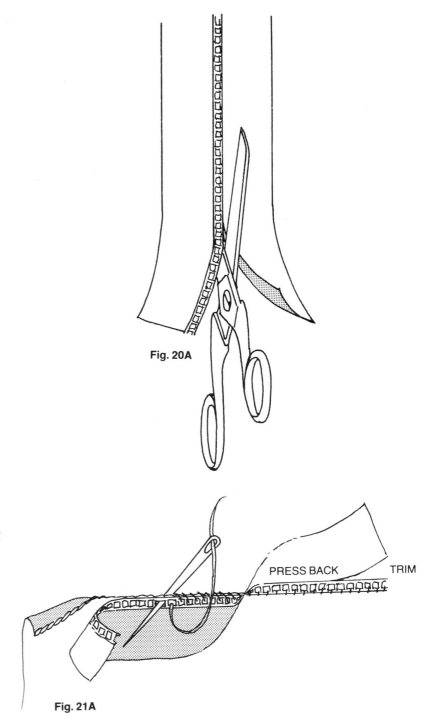

Fig. 20A

PRESS BACK   TRIM

Fig. 21A

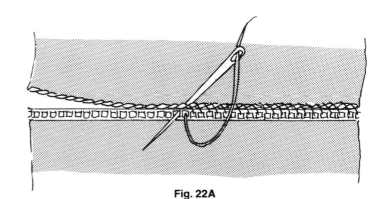

Fig. 22A

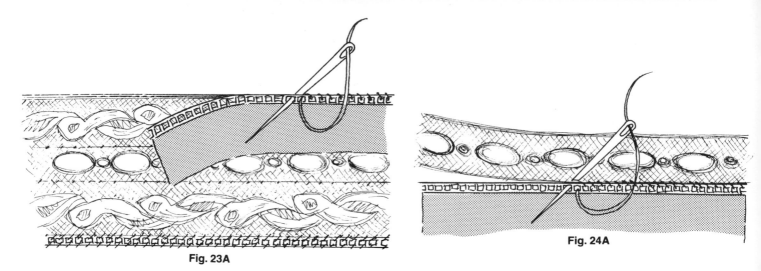

Fig. 23A

Fig. 24A

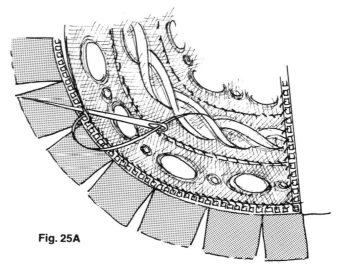

Fig. 25A

JOINING ENTREDEUX INTO A CIRCLE

Start sewing the entredeux even with a seam and sew back to the original seam, overlapping two (2) holes to join. (See Figures 26A and 27A.) Press back and trim the other side.

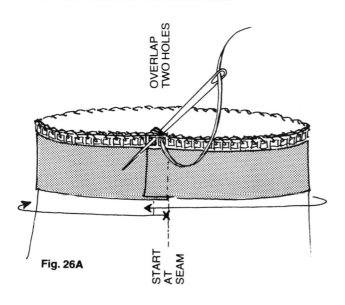

OVERLAP TWO HOLES

Fig. 26A

START AT SEAM

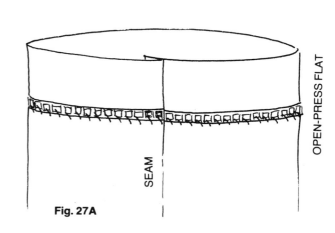

Fig. 27A

SEAM

OPEN-PRESS FLAT

MITERING ENTREDEUX

Without Cutting

Sew the entredeux to the point where it is to be mitered and clip the fabric as shown in Figure 28A. Fold one (1) hole under the other to make the point. (See Figure 29A.)

By Cutting

Sew the entredeux to a point. Leave one (1) hole extended beyond the point and cut entredeux off. (See Figure 30A.) Overlap one (1) hole over the extended one and whip together. (See Figure 31A.)

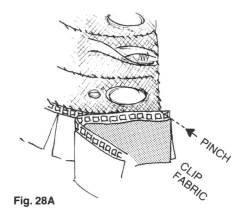

Fig. 28A

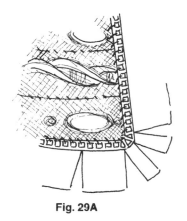

Fig. 29A

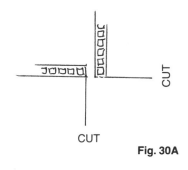

CUT

Fig. 30A

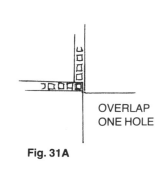

OVERLAP
ONE HOLE

Fig. 31A

APPLICATION OF ENTREDEUX TO LACE

Generally, the entredeux is sewn to material and then the lace is added to the entredeux because lace has a tendency to stretch and material does not. An exception to the rule of applying the entredeux to the material would be when joining a ruffle or lace edge to a band of lace insertion on the bottom of a garment, such as a skirt. (See Figure 32A.)

NOTE: It is advisable to measure the entredeux to be the same size as the bottom of the garment to which it is to be applied, and to pin it to the lace band in fourths before sewing right sides together.

Fig. 32A

Starting a thread without a knot when joining lace to lace, lace to entredeux or lace or entredeux to a rolled edge.

Pass the needle from the back to the front leaving a short tail of thread. (See Figure 33A.)

Hold the tail of the thread and insert the needle once again halfway and wrap the single thread three or four times clockwise around the needle. (See Figure 34A.)

Gently hold the wraps with the left thumb and pull the needle through the twists of thread until it forms a tight knot. (See Figure 35A.)

Clip the short tail of thread. (See Figure 36A.)

Proceed with the whip stitch.

Ending a thread when joining lace to lace, lace to entredeux or lace or entredeux to a rolled edge.

Insert the needle from the back to the front without pulling it completely through.

Wrap the single thread three or four times clockwise around the needle. (See Figure 37A.)

Gently hold the wraps with the left thumb and pull the needle through the twists of thread until it forms a tight knot. (See Figure 38A.)

Clip thread. (See Figure 39A.)

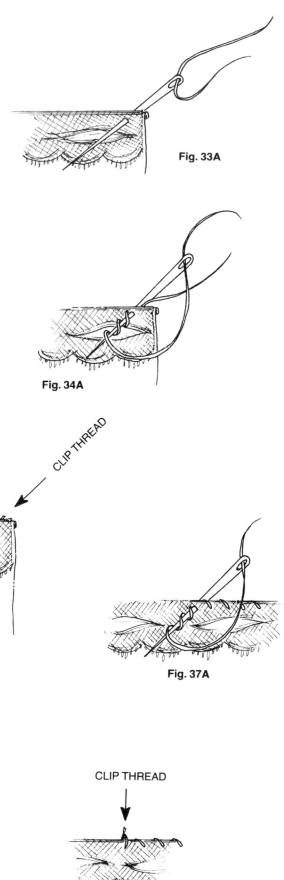

Fig. 33A

Fig. 34A

CLIP THREAD

Fig. 36A

Fig. 37A

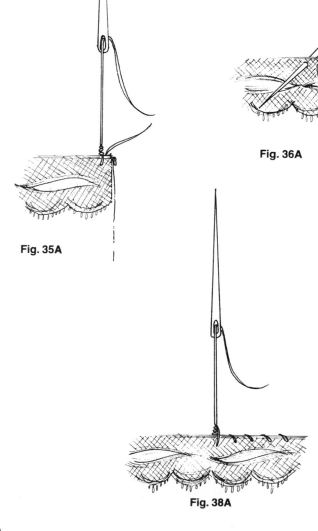

Fig. 35A

Fig. 38A

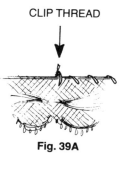

CLIP THREAD

Fig. 39A

22

APPLICATION OF LACE TO A ROLLED EDGE

Lay the right side of the lace to the right side of the rolled edge with the top edges even and, whipping over and over, go under the roll and through the lace, taking up the heavy line on the lace. Stitches should be 1/8 inch apart. (See Figure 40A.)

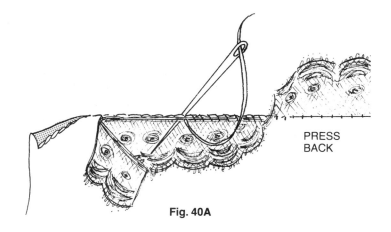

PRESS
BACK

Fig. 40A

APPLICATION OF LACE TO LACE

Lay the right sides of the two lengths of lace together and, whipping over and over, go under the heavy line, pulling tight enough so that the two laces look to be one when pressed back. (See Figure 41A.)

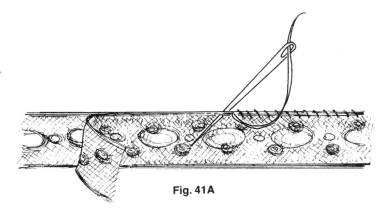

Fig. 41A

APPLICATION OF LACE SIDE BY SIDE

With the right sides of the laces face down on a paper guide, baste each row of lace to the paper, butting the edges together, but not overlapping them. Whip together, taking up the heavy line on each side. Be sure to pull the thread taut so that the laces appear to be one piece of lace. (See Figure 42A.)

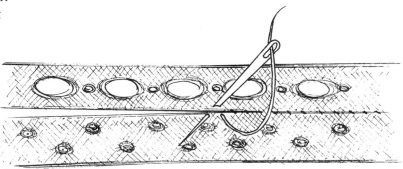

Fig. 42A

GATHER LACE TO RUFFLE

Pick up one (1) of the threads forming the heavy line on the edge of the lace and gently pull in order to gather. In some laces the thread will not pull; it is then necessary to put in a running stitch by hand or machine. Lace is generally gathered one and one-half (1½) times for fullness. (See Figure 43A.)

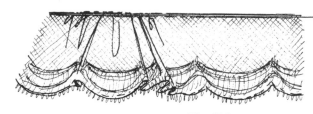

Fig. 43A

APPLICATION OF LACE TO ENTREDEUX
(Gathered or Flat)

Lay the right side of the lace to the right side of the entredeux with the top edges even and, whipping over and over, go through the entredeux hole, taking up the heavy line on the lace. (See Figure 44A.)

NOTE: Adjust gathers on lace as you whip. (See Figure 45A.)

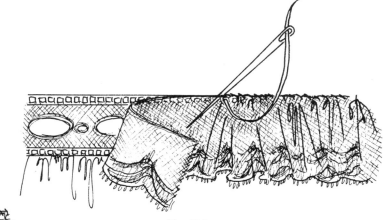

Fig. 45A

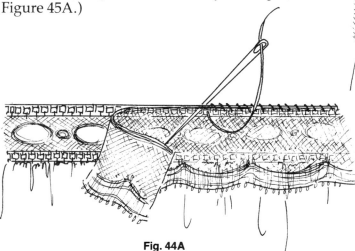

Fig. 44A

JOINING LACE ON A CURVE

Lace may be shaped into a curve or circle by pulling a thread in the heading of the lace in order to gather the top side just enough that the bottom edge will lie flat without puckering. It is basted to the paper, side by side, with the right side facing the paper, and then whipped together by taking up the heavy lines. (See Figure 46A.)

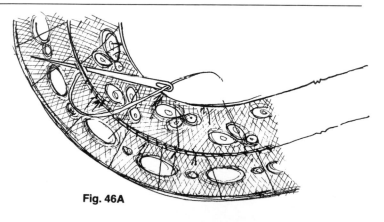

Fig. 46A

JOINING LACE TOGETHER AT SEAM

Joining by buttonhole stitch.

Extend the lace 1/4 inch beyond seam line. (See Figure 47A.) Start attaching lace by whipping at the seam line and continue back to the starting point, leaving another 1/4 inch of lace loose. Fold the first 1/4 inch back even with the seam so that it overlaps the ending 1/4 inch. (See figure 48A.) Baste the seam on the right side with tiny stitches. (See figure 49A.) Work a fine buttonhole stitch as close to the fold as possible on the right side. (See Figure 50A.) Trim the excess lace as close as possible on the wrong side. (See Figure 51A.)

Joining by rolling and whipping.

This method does not give the fine appearance that buttonholing does, but some prefer to use it. The two loose ends may be joined by rolling and whipping together on the wrong side. They should be rolled and whipped even with the seam as shown in Figures 52A, 53A, and 54A.

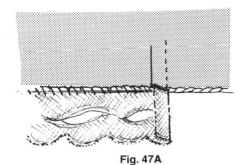

Fig. 47A

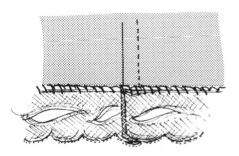

Fig. 48A

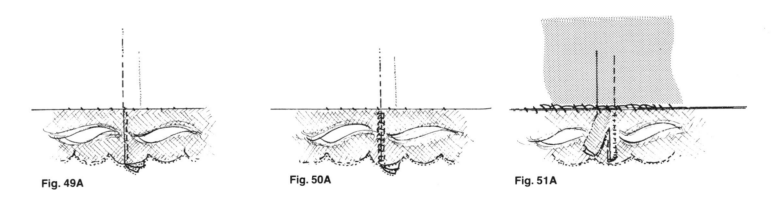

Fig. 49A

Fig. 50A

Fig. 51A

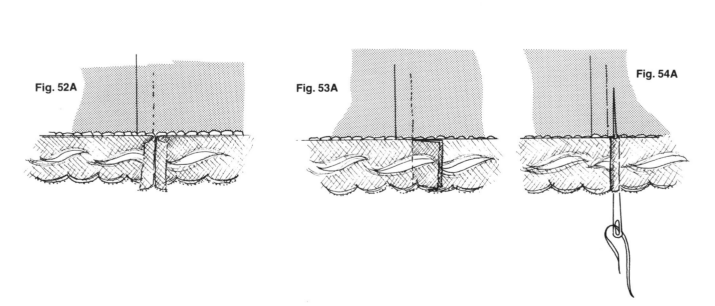

Fig. 52A

Fig. 53A

Fig. 54A

JOINING STRAIGHT STRIPS
OF LACE TOGETHER

Joining by buttonhole stitch.

Fold back 1/4 inch of one (1) end of the lace and lap over the other end of the lace. Baste and buttonhole stitch as close to the fold as possible. Trim excess lace away. (See Figure 55A.)

Joining by rolling and whipping.

Bring the raw edges of the lace together (right side to right side) tiny baste and, laying the needle in a horizontal position, firmly hold the needle and lace, and roll one complete roll or approximately 1/4 inch. Pull the needle out of the roll and proceed to join by rolling and whipping. (See Figure 56A.)

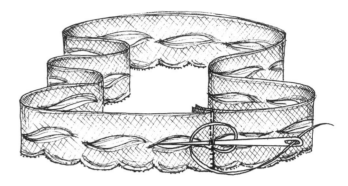

Fig. 55A

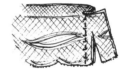

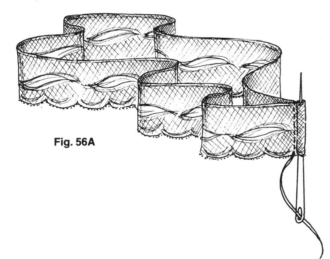

Fig. 56A

MITERED LACE

Start sewing the lace at one corner, leaving the width of the lace extending beyond the edge. (See Figure 57A.) (Example: If the lace is one (1) inch wide, leave one (1) inch loose. If the lace is two (2) inches wide leave two (2) inches loose.)

Sew to the next corner and extend the lace its width; fold back and double. (See Figure 58A.)

Sew at an angle on the wrong side, as shown in Figure 59A.

Tiny baste on top as shown in Figure 60A.

Buttonhole the miter on the right side as close to the fold as possible. (See Figure 61A.)

Trim away excess lace on the wrong side. (See Figure 62A.)

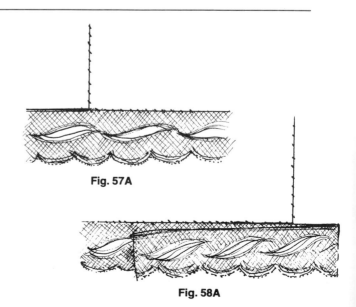

Fig. 57A

Fig. 58A

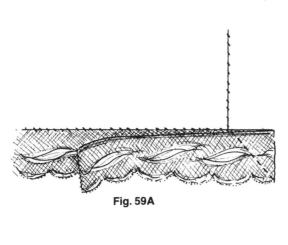

Fig. 59A

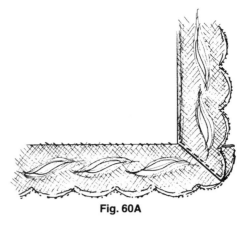

Fig. 60A

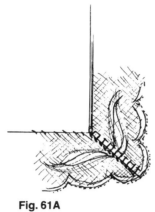

Fig. 61A

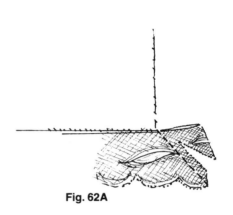

Fig. 62A

MITERED EYELET

Eyelet is mitered in the same way as lace; however, it is finished off differently:

Baste the angle at the corner on the wrong side.

Machine stitch three (3) times over the basting, one line of stitching on top of the other. (See Figure 63A.)

Trim the excess fabric away 1/8 inch from stitching line. (See Figure 63A.)

Finish the raw edge with an overcast stitch or by rolling and whipping. (See Figures 64A and 65A.)

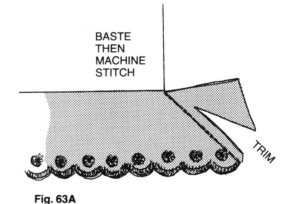

BASTE
THEN
MACHINE
STITCH

TRIM

Fig. 63A

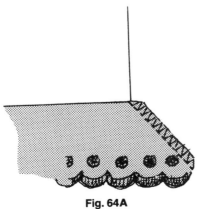

Fig. 64A

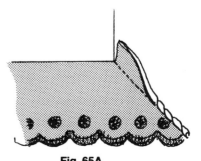

Fig. 65A

APPLICATION OF LACE OR RUFFLES TO A FINISHED EDGE

Yoke

Start the lace at the placket edge on the back yoke. (See Figure 66A.) Lay the right side of the lace up on the yoke and catch, by whipping, to the gathers (on the skirt and sleeve just below the entredeux). (See 66A Detail.) The lace will then turn back. Gather the lace fuller at the corners so it will turn without cupping. (See Figure 67A.) Ruffles may be attached in the same way.

Crown of a Bonnet or Cap

Star the lace at a given point on the circle by laying the right side of the lace up on the circle. Catch, by whipping, to the gathers on the puff. The lace will then turn back and the entredeux will show. (See Figure 68A.)

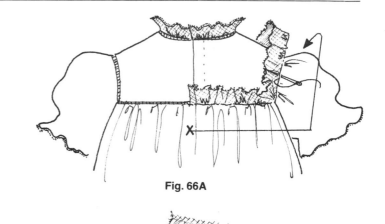

Fig. 66A

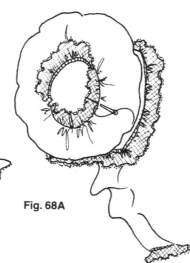

Fig. 68A

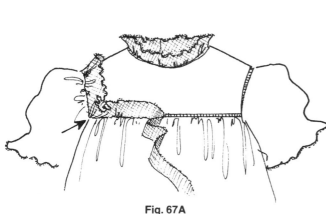

Fig. 67A

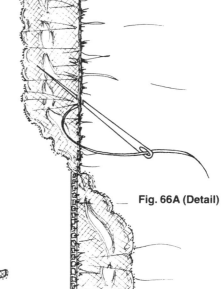

Fig. 66A (Detail)

FINISHING LACE AT NECK EDGE

Leave 1/4 inch of lace extending beyond the placket edge on each end. (See Figure 69A.)

Roll and whip the lace even with the placket. (See Figure 70A.)

This same method may be applied to lace that forms a ruffle around a yoke and to the lace applied to the end of streamers.

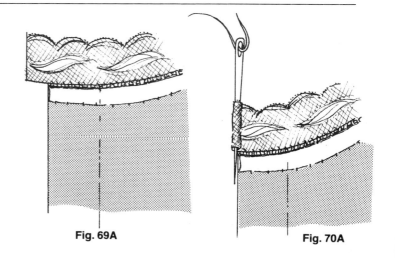

Fig. 69A

Fig. 70A

BLINDSTITCH

Turn the raw edge of the material under the desired amount (usually about 1/4 inch).

Press and baste.

Run the needle 1/4 inch inside the material fold and bring needle and thread out again. (See Figure 71A.)

Pick up one (1) or two (2) threads on the single fabric and pull the thread down firmly. (See Figure 72A.)

Repeat process.

This stitch is used for whipping plackets, hemming, and whipping bias bindings.

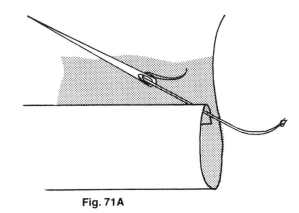

Fig. 71A

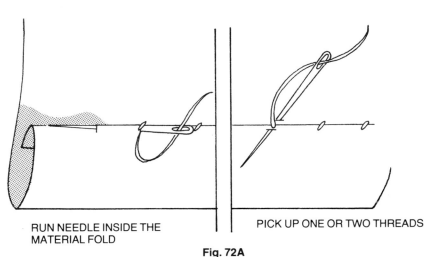

RUN NEEDLE INSIDE THE MATERIAL FOLD

PICK UP ONE OR TWO THREADS

Fig. 72A

MAKING A BUTTONHOLE

Place the button on the material where the buttonhole is needed. Indicate the size of the buttonhole by marking the fabric on each side of the button with a pencil dot or silk pins. (See Figure 73A).

Fold material in center of buttonhole and cut from the folded edge to the mark. (See Figure 74A.)

With a knotted thread, take a stitch going from the right side under to the bottom left side of the opening, and pull the thread through. (See Figure 75A.)

Work the first side of the buttonhole by looping the thread up and around, inserting the needle from the opening into the material, and taking a stitch the width buttonhole is to be. (See Figure 76A.)

Sew to the top left side of the opening. (See Figure 77A.)

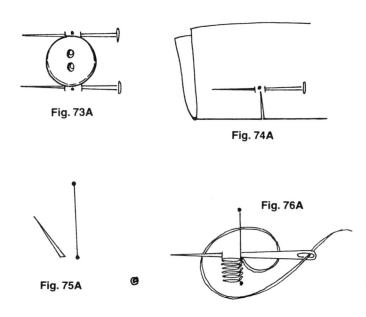

Fig. 73A

Fig. 74A

Fig. 75A

Fig. 76A

Bar tac the ends with two stitches. (See Figure 78A.)

Insert the needle at the outer point of the second stitch and bring the needle and thread back through the opening. (See Figure 78A.)

Turn the buttonhole upside down and repeat the rest of the steps as shown in Figures 79A and 80A.

Run the needle and thread under the stitching line to secure, and cut off the beginning knot. (See Figure 81A.)

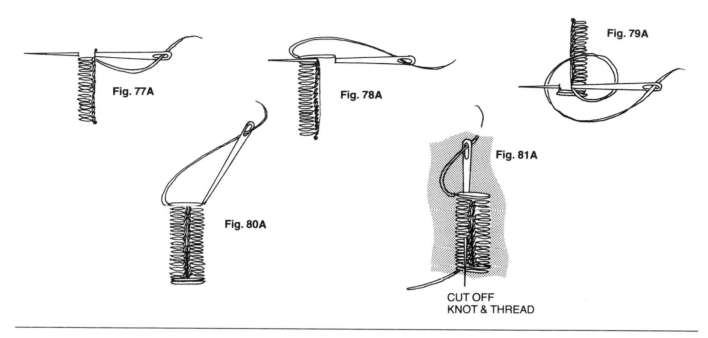

Fig. 77A

Fig. 78A

Fig. 79A

Fig. 80A

Fig. 81A

CUT OFF
KNOT & THREAD

CONTINUOUS PLACKET

The method of application for continuous plackets is identical to that for Bishop or Raglan sleeve dresses, yoked dresses, and sleeve openings where a cuff is used. The only difference is the length of the placket (generally three (3) inches for a child's yoke dress, six (6) to seven (7) inches for a Bishop or Raglan sleeve dress, and two and one-half (2½) to three (3) inches for a sleeve.)

Cut the opening for the placket the desired length. (See Figure 82A.)

Cut a straight strip of material 1½ inches wide and long enough to go around the entire opening.

Pull the slit into a straight line. (See Figure 83A.)

Lay the right side of the strip to the right side of the placket slit and sew from 1/8 inch to the point of the slit, and from the point to 1/8 inch on the other side. (See Figure 84A.)

Press seam toward placket strip.

Turn the raw edge under enough to finish 1/2 inch wide and lay the fold edge on top of the

Fig. 82A

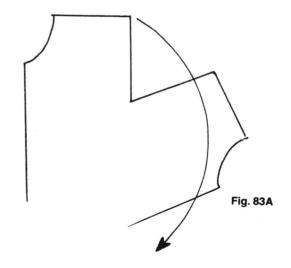

Fig. 83A

stitching line. Baste and then blindstitch.

Turn the side of the placket that is to lap to the wrong side and secure with tiny basting stitches across the top. (See Figure 86A.)

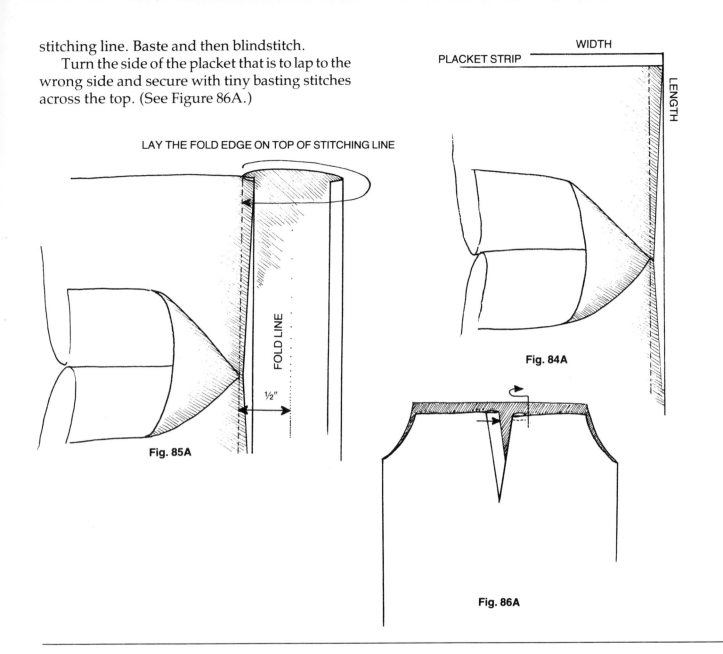

LAY THE FOLD EDGE ON TOP OF STITCHING LINE

FOLD LINE

½"

Fig. 85A

PLACKET STRIP

WIDTH

LENGTH

Fig. 84A

Fig. 86A

CONCEALED NECK BINDING

This type of binding is used to attach most collars permanently to the neck edge of a garment. It is also used to finish a neck edge on which a detachable collar might be used.

Cut a bias strip of fabric 1/2 inch, plus (+) the width of the seam allowance, times (×) the neck measurement of the garment from fold line to fold line. (See Figure 87A.)

Lay the collar on the yoke with the outer edge even with the center back line. (If attaching a split collar, the centers should meet in the front, but should not overlap.) (See Figure 88A.)

Turn the placket back on the fold line over the collar. Pin or baste securely. Lay the bias strip on top of the placket and baste to the neck edge on the seam line. Sew with tiny running stitches or

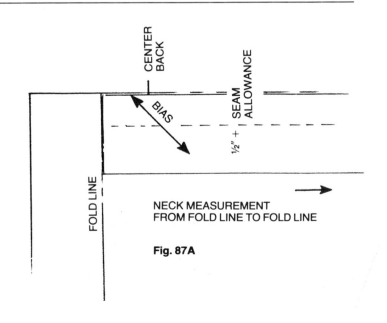

CENTER BACK

BIAS

SEAM ALLOWANCE

½" +

FOLD LINE

NECK MEASUREMENT FROM FOLD LINE TO FOLD LINE

Fig. 87A

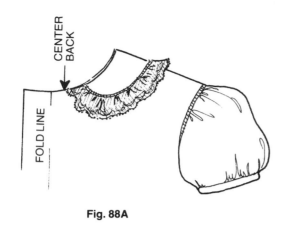

Fig. 88A

machine stitch the entire neck edge, from end to end. (See Figure 89A.)

Trim the fabric on top to 1/4 inch of the stitching line.

Turn the placket right side out with the bias strip folding to the inside. (See Figure 90A.)

Turn the raw edge of the bias strip under 1/4 inch. Baste, and then blindstitch. (See Figure 91A.)

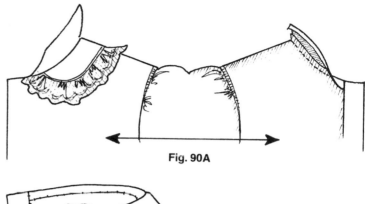

Fig. 90A

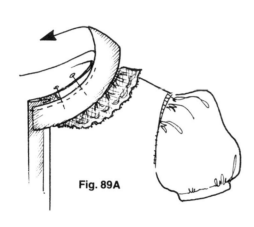

Fig. 89A

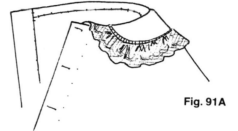

Fig. 91A

EXPOSED NECK BINDING

This type of binding is used to attach smocked collars and to finish dresses where a collar is not used, such as smocked bishop dresses.

Cut a bias strip of fabric 1/2 inch wide, plus (+) the width of the seam allowance, times (×) the neck measurement (including the extended placket), plus (+) 1/2 inch. (See Figure 92A.)

Pin the edge of the binding to the top edge of the neck with right sides together, leaving 1/4 inch extending beyond each end.

Sew the binding to the neck of the garment on the seam allowance.

Press binding up and trim, leaving approximately 1/8 inch above the stitching line. (See Figure 93A.)

Fold the extending ends to the wrong side, even with the back neck edges, and press.

Fold the top raw edge under 1/4 inch before turning to the inside of the garment and blindstitching over the seam. (See Figure 94A.)

Blindstitch the ends of the neck binding.

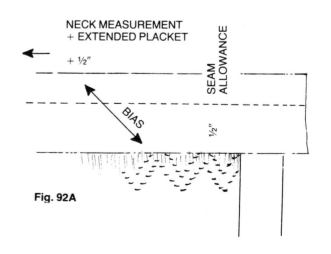

NECK MEASUREMENT
+ EXTENDED PLACKET

+ ½"

SEAM ALLOWANCE

BIAS

½"

Fig. 92A

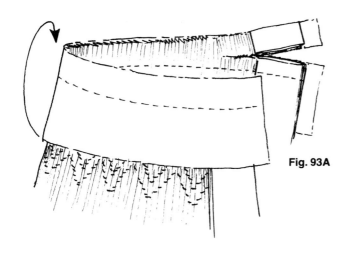

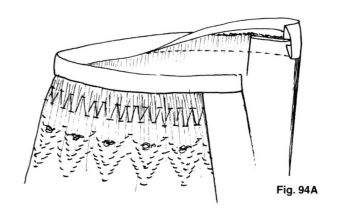

Fig. 93A

Fig. 94A

ENTREDEUX APPLIED AS A BINDING

This method is used when the material cannot be rolled and whipped (smocking, puffing, and sometimes, tucks):

Trim the fabric away from one side of the entredeux.

Lay the trimmed side of the entredeux down from the neck edge, right sides together. (See Figure 95A.)

Baste the fabric on the entredeux to the fabric of the garment, as close to the entredeux holes as possible.

Sew with tiny running stitches or machine stitch over basting stitches. (See Figure 95A.)

Fold the trimmed side of the entredeux up. Cut away the heavy fabric from behind the entredeux fabric. DO NOT CUT THE ENTREDEUX FABRIC. (See Figure 96A.)

Turn the raw edge of the entredeux fabric under 1/8 inch. Baste and blindstitch. (See Figure 97A.)

Lace edging (gathered or flat) may now be whipped to the entredeux.

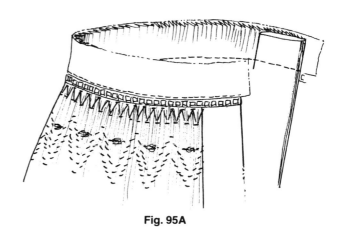

Fig. 95A

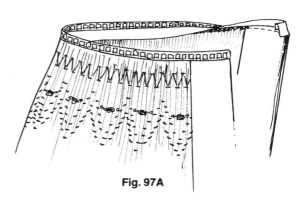

Fig. 97A

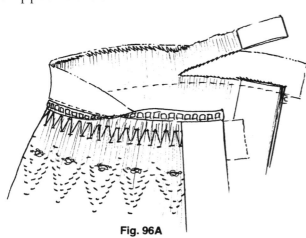

Fig. 96A

MAKING COLLARS DETACHABLE

Collars with a lace neck edge

Cut a strip of lace insertion or net footing 1/4 to 1/2 inch wide and 1/2 inch longer than the neck measurement (from center back to center back) of the garment that the collar will be attached to.

Roll and whip or fold lace under 1/4 inch to the wrong side on each end. (See Figure 98A.)

Whip the binding lace to the top edge of the collar (including the lace edging), in equal halves, with right sides together.

Sew the binding lace to the inside of the finished neck edge of the garment. (See Figure 100A.)

Collars with a fabric neck edge

Cut a bias strip of fabric 3/4 inch wide and 1/2 inch longer than the neck measurement (from center back to center back) of the garment that the collar will be attached to.

Fold each end of the bias strip 1/4 inch to the wrong side and press.

Pin the fabric binding (with the right sides together) to the neck edge of the collar, including the lace edging, in equal halves. Sew by hand or machine 1/4 inch from neck edge. (See Figure 101A.)

Press seam toward raw edge of binding. Fold edge of binding under 1/4 inch and lay on the stitching line at neck. Baste and then blindstitch. Whip ends of binding. Sew the binding to the inside of the finished neck edge of garment. (See Figure 103A.)

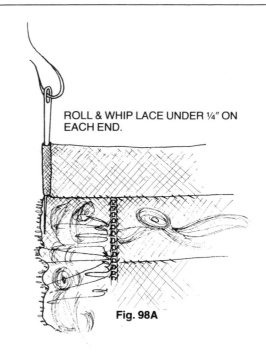

ROLL & WHIP LACE UNDER ¼" ON EACH END.

Fig. 98A

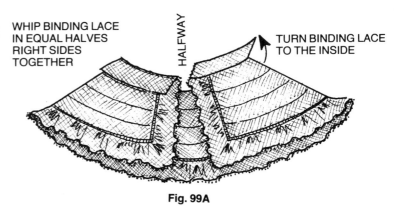

WHIP BINDING LACE IN EQUAL HALVES RIGHT SIDES TOGETHER

HALFWAY

TURN BINDING LACE TO THE INSIDE

Fig. 99A

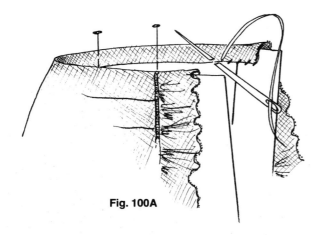

Fig. 100A

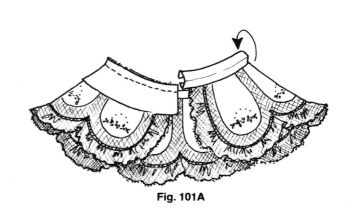

Fig. 101A

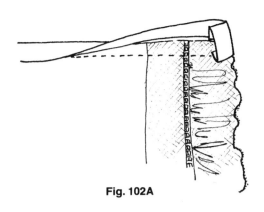

Fig. 102A

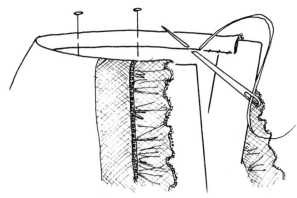

Fig. 103A

HEM BELOW FANCY BAND

Cut strips of fabric following measurements for desired size.

French seam the strips to form 1 large circle. Roll and whip one edge.

Whip entredeux to the rolled edge. (See Figure 104.)

Join the fancy band to the entredeux.

Pin the band to the entredeux on top of hem in equal fourths and then whip to the entredeux.

Turn the bottom edge of the fabric up 1/4 inch and press.

Fold hem in half and whip to the rolled edge just under the entredeux. (See Figure 105.)

See chart for hem measurements for children's dresses.

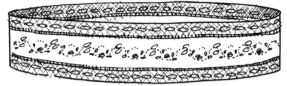

JOIN THE FANCY BAND TO THE ENTREDEUX

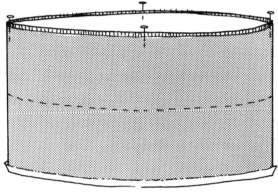

Fig. 104A

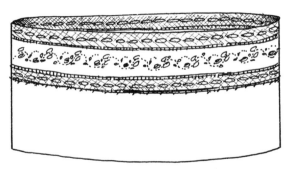

Fig. 105A

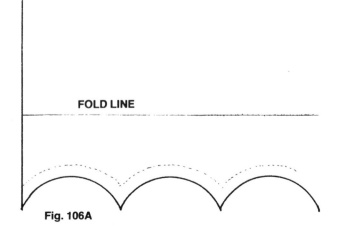

FOLD LINE

Fig. 106A

SHAPED HEM

Divide the bottom width of the skirt into equal sections.

Draw design (scallops or points) on the bottom edge of the skirt, 1/2 inch up from the raw edge. (See Figure 106A.)

Trim, leaving 1/8 inch of fabric to turn under and tiny baste. (See Figure 107A.)

Fold hem up and baste again. (See Figure 108A.)

Feather stitch hem on the right side, taking one (1) stitch on the hem and one (1) stitch on the skirt. (See Figure 108A.)

The points of the design may be embellished with an embroidery motif. (See Figure 108A or 109A.)

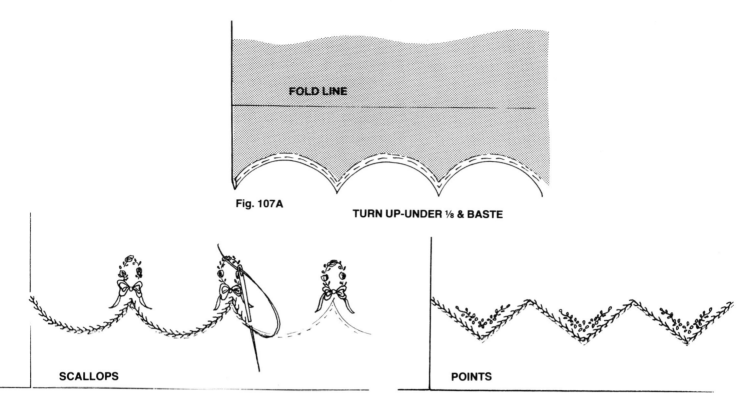

Fig. 107A

FOLD LINE

TURN UP-UNDER ⅛ & BASTE

SCALLOPS

Fig. 108A

POINTS

Fig. 109A

SHELL HEM

This stitch makes a lovely finish on children's underwear (especially for the neck and arm-holes). It can be used instead of entredeux and lace.

Begin by making a double 1/8 inch hem. It is easier to baste the hem in before working the shell stitch.

Secure the thread at the starting point, hiding the knot inside the fold. Slip the needle back in the fold and bring needle and thread out 1/8 inch away. Pick up one (1) or two (2) threads and pull thread taunt.

Repeat, but this time, throw the needle and thread over the hem (at the same place the second stitch has been taken) and bring the needle through the base of the hem and through the loop the thread forms. Pull tight, forming the shell. (See Figure 113A.)

Alternate two (2) blind stitches and a shell stitch. (See Figures 110A, 111A and 112A.)

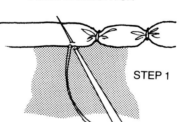

FIRST BLINDSTITCH

STEP 1

Fig. 110A

SECOND BLINDSTITCH

STEP 2

Fig. 111A

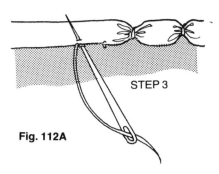

PICK UP ONE OR TWO THREADS

STEP 3

Fig. 112A

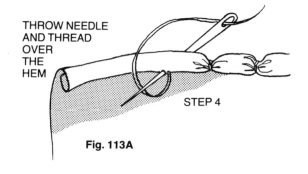

THROW NEEDLE
AND THREAD
OVER
THE
HEM

STEP 4

Fig. 113A

SLEEVE STITCH

THIS STITCH, KNOWN AS "SARAH'S STITCH," WAS DESIGNED TO FORM A SOFT RUFFLE WHEN BEADING AND RIBBON ARE NOT DESIRED.

Measure up one (1) inch from the entredeux on the bottom of the sleeve and in one and one-half (1½) inches from either side and make a crease or mark with light pencil dots. (See Figure 114A.)

Thread needle with a **very long** single thread (approximately two (2) yards long) and knot the end.

Sew from A to B on the crease with tiny running stitches. (See Figure 115A.)

Lay the needle 1/4 inch below B at C and sew back to D. (See Figure 116A.)

Take the knotted end of the thread and the thread in the needle and pull at the same time in order to gather the sleeve to the proper size. (See Figure 117A.) Tie the two threads together (as many times as needed), making a knot that does not slip. (See Figure 118A.)

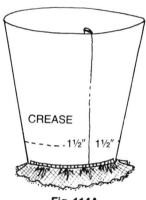

CREASE

1½" 1½"

Fig. 114A

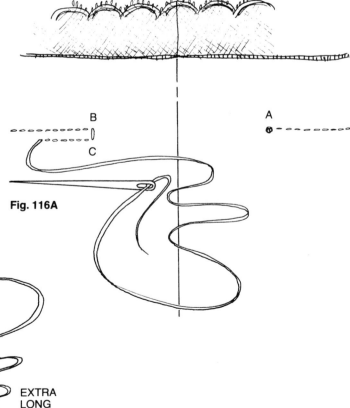

B

A

C

Fig. 116A

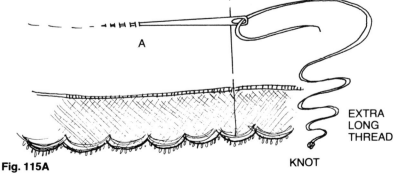

A

EXTRA
LONG
THREAD

Fig. 115A

KNOT

Pull the short thread in the needle down further than the thread that is secured in the fabric and take one small stitch, making the thread come up double. (See Figure 119A.)

Tie the double threads together, making a knot that does not slip. Clip the short threads off. You now have a long, double thread with which to sew.

Work the fancy stitch between the two gathering stitches, as shown in Figure 120A. The needle should always go from right to left under the stitching line.

Adjust gathers as you stitch.

Right Stitch — Let the thread lay straight down and take the right stitch.

Left Stitch — Loop the thread down and to the left to take the left stitch.

Always pull the thread at an angle toward the stitch you have just made.

When you reach the end, knot the thread with a slip knot several times before taking the needle and thread to the underside. (See Figure 121A.) Clip the thread close to the eye of the needle, leaving double threads to split and tie together several times. Clip excess thread off.

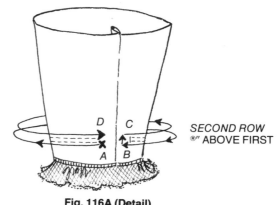

Fig. 116A (Detail)

SECOND ROW
⑧" ABOVE FIRST

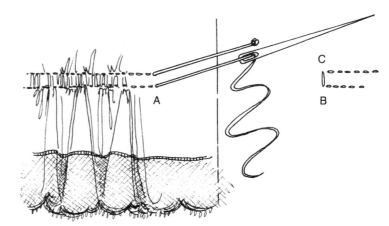

Fig. 117A

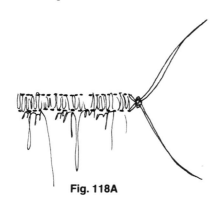

Fig. 118A

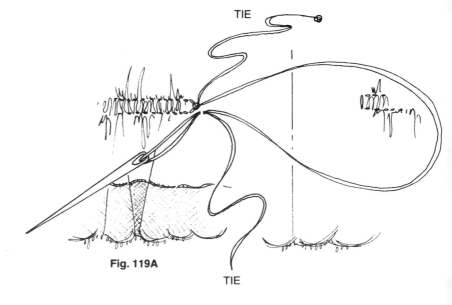

TIE

TIE

Fig. 119A

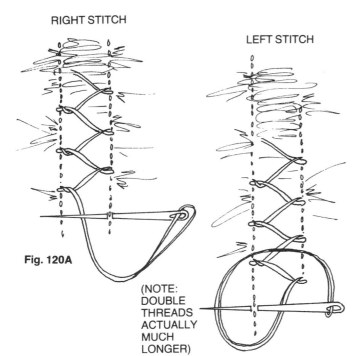

RIGHT STITCH

LEFT STITCH

Fig. 120A

(NOTE: DOUBLE THREADS ACTUALLY MUCH LONGER)

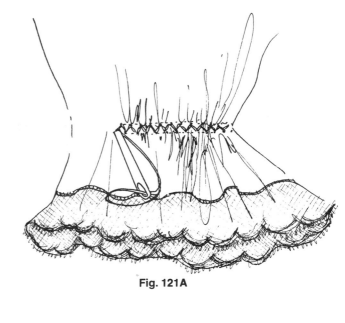

Fig. 121A

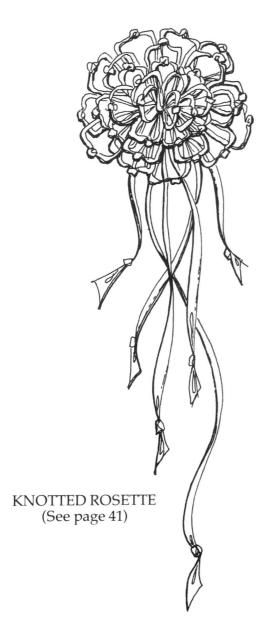

KNOTTED ROSETTE
(See page 41)

ROSETTES

Rosettes are an elegant addition to caps and bonnets. Both small and large rosettes are made from one (1) inch, double-face satin ribbon. (See Figure 122A.)

SMALL ROSETTES

Cut a nine and one-half (9½) inch length of ribbon. Measure 1/4 inch from the top left end and make a light pencil dot. From this dot, make nine (9) more dots one (1) inch apart, thus leaving 1/4 inch on the right top side. Make nine (9) dots on the bottom of the ribbon, spaced halfway between the top dots. (See Figure 123A.)

LARGE ROSETTES

Cut a twenty-seven and one-half (27½) inch length of ribbon. Measure in 1/4 inch from the top left end and make a pencil dot. From this dot, make twelve (12) more dots two and one-fourth (2¼) inches apart, thus leaving 1/4 inch on the right top side. Make twelve (12) dots on the bottom of the ribbon, spaced halfway between the top dots. (See Figure 124A.)

GENERAL INSTRUCTIONS

With a knotted single thread, connect the dots, with a large basting stitch, to form triangles as shown in Figures 123A and 124A. Leave the needle and thread dangling when you reach the end. Bring the ends of the ribbon together, forming a circle, and with another needle and double thread, sew tiny running stitches along the 1/4 inch seam allowance. See Figure 125A.

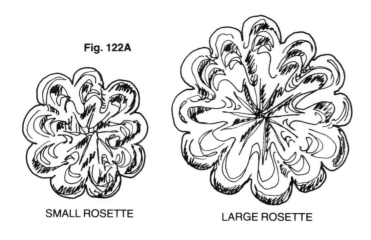

Fig. 122A

SMALL ROSETTE · · · LARGE ROSETTE

Pull the original thread in order to gather the ribbon and form a rosette. (See Figure 125A.) With the needle and thread, go through each point of the triangle on the inside and pull the center together. (See Figure 126A.) Whip back and forth on the wrong side to secure. Turn all edges on the outer side of the rosette to the wrong side.

Sew the rosette to the garment, coming up between a fold and going directly back down in the same place. Sew around the entire rosette in this manner, working first inside, and then, the outer edge.

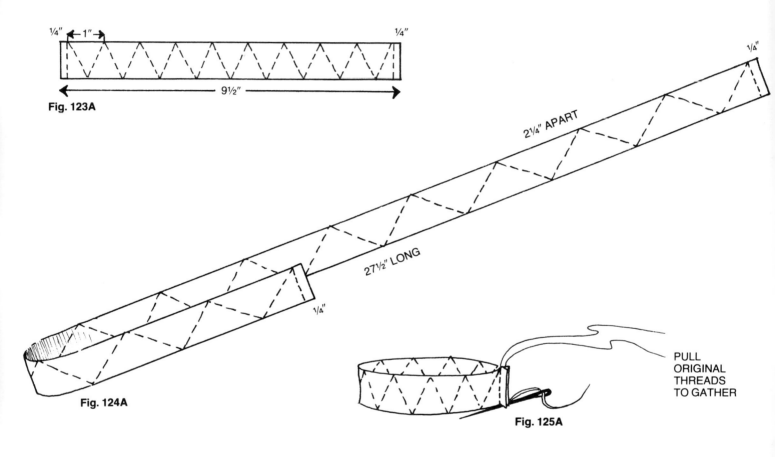

¼" ← 1" → ¼"   ¼"

9½"

Fig. 123A

2¼" APART

27½" LONG

¼"

Fig. 124A

PULL ORIGINAL THREADS TO GATHER

Fig. 125A

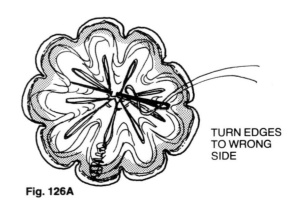

TURN EDGES TO WRONG SIDE

Fig. 126A

KNOTTED ROSETTES

Knotted rosettes are made from 1/8 inch or 1/4 inch double-faced satin ribbon.

For the large rosettes make forty (40) knots two and one-half (2½) inches apart and for the small rosette, twenty-five (25) knots two (2) inches apart.

Take a stitch half way between the end of the ribbon and the first knot, bringing the knot on the top of the finger of the left hand. (See Figure 127A.) Continue in like manner until you have half of the knots threaded on the needle. (See Figure 128A.) Pull the needle and thread completely through, sliding the knots down toward the knot of the thread.

Thread the remaining half of the ribbon knots on the needle and thread through, sliding all of the knots together compactly in a straight line. (See Figure 129A.)

Loop the ends together. Stitch to secure. (See Figure 130A.)

Streamers may be made, if desired, and sewn on the back of the knotted rosette.

USE DOUBLE THREAD

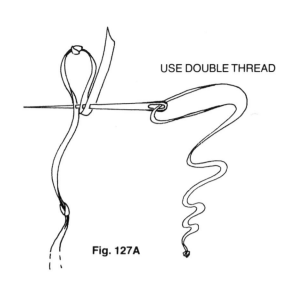

Fig. 127A

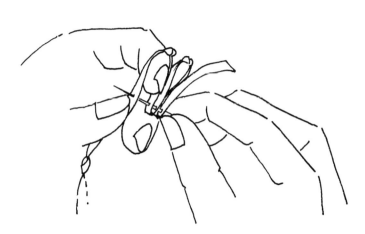

Fig. 128A

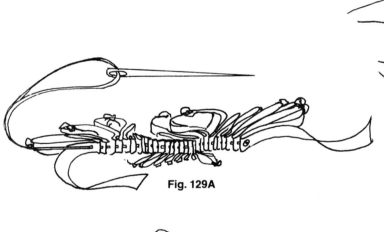

Fig. 129A

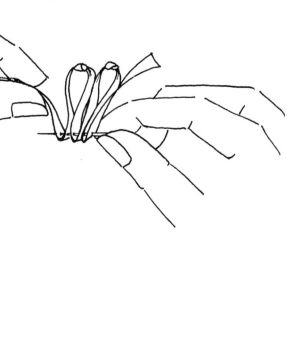

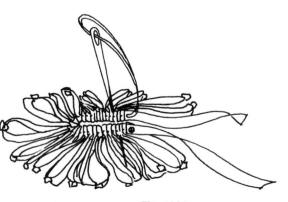

Fig. 130A

Basic Ruffle Instructions

Pull and cut the number of strips for ruffle depth needed, times (×) the width. (Ruffles are generally one and one-half (1½) to two (2) times the measurement for fullness, depending upon their use.

French seam the strips to form one large circle. Make seams 1/8 inch wide each time.
NOTE: Start the next three steps at one given seam. (See Figure 131A.) Roll and whip the bottom edge.

Whip entredeux to the rolled bottom edge.

Whip an appropriate trim or trims to the entredeux.

Joining a Ruffle To a Skirt or Fancy Band

Fourth (¼) the ruffle letting the seam where the lace is joined be center back — mark each fourth (¼) with a pin or colored thread loop.

Fourth (¼) the bottom of the skirt or band — mark each fourth (¼) with a pin or colored thread loop.

Pin one-fourth (¼) of the ruffle to one-fourth (¼) of the skirt or band.

Join the ruffle to the entredeux on the bottom of the skirt or band by rolling and whipping the top of the ruffle in equal fourths (¼'s) to fit equal fourths (¼s) of the skirt or band.

Whip the rolled edge to the entredeux with another needle and thread. (See Figure 132A.)

RUFFLES

1/4   1/4

1/4   1/4

Fig. 131A

START HERE

ATTACH RUFFLE IN 1/4ths

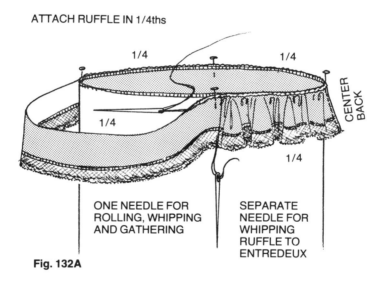

1/4   1/4

1/4

1/4

CENTER BACK

ONE NEEDLE FOR ROLLING, WHIPPING AND GATHERING

SEPARATE NEEDLE FOR WHIPPING RUFFLE TO ENTREDEUX

Fig. 132A

TUCKS

TUCKS

Tucks are used to embellish French handsewn creations, whether baby dresses, pillows, or blouses for adults. They are especially appropriate for little boys' clothing.

Tucks are exactly what the name implies, folds sewn in material. They may vary in size from being no wider than a needle to being more than two inches wide.

Straightness is achieved by pulling a thread in order to form a guideline by which to fold the material. (See Figures 1B, 2B, 3B, 4B.) Or, if the tuck is wide, the pulled thread will serve as a guideline to sew on. (See Figures 5B, 6B, 7B.)

Let your imagination soar and see what lovely heirlooms you can create with tucks.

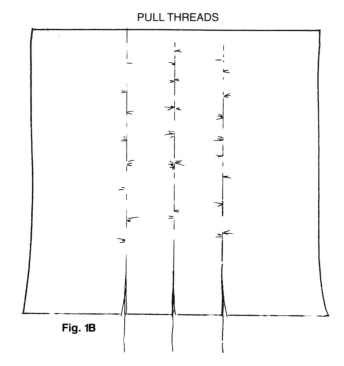

PULL THREADS

Fig. 1B

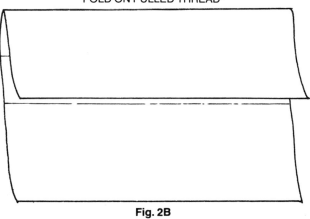

FOLD ON PULLED THREAD

Fig. 2B

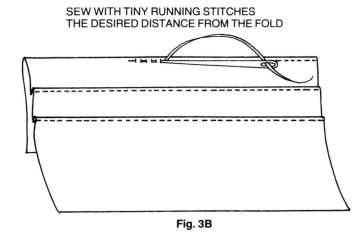

SEW WITH TINY RUNNING STITCHES
THE DESIRED DISTANCE FROM THE FOLD

Fig. 3B

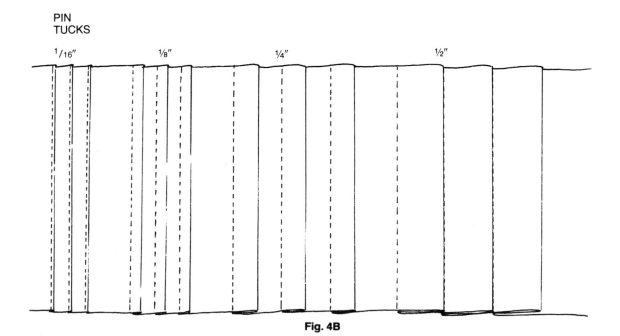

PIN
TUCKS

1/16"   1/8"   1/4"   1/2"

Fig. 4B

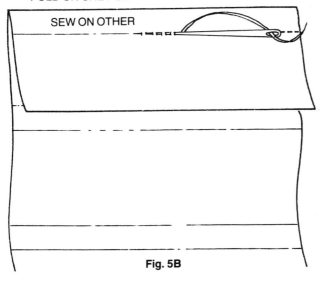

FOLD ON ONE PULLED THREAD

SEW ON OTHER

Fig. 5B

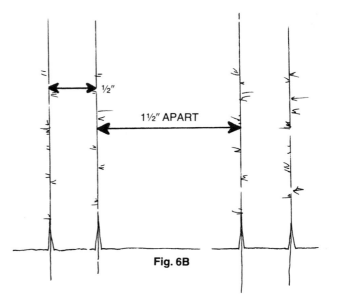

½"

1½" APART

Fig. 6B

TUCKED STRIPS

Tucked strips may be cut the desired length, or one long strip may be tucked and then cut into strips of whatever length is needed. The strip must be wide enough to accommodate the number of tucks wanted, leaving at least 3/4 inch on either side for rolling and whipping or for applying lace insertion.

Fold the fabric on each pulled thread and sew, with tiny running stitches, the desired width from the folded edge. Press tucks the direction you want them to go.

To cut, measure the length of the strip needed and machine stitch across the tucks. Skip 1/8 inch and machine stitch again. Cut between the two stitching lines. These strips may be inserted in a garment vertically, horizontally, or diagonally. (See Figure 8B.)

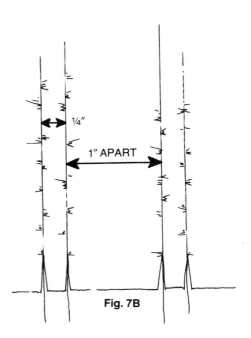

¼"

1" APART

Fig. 7B

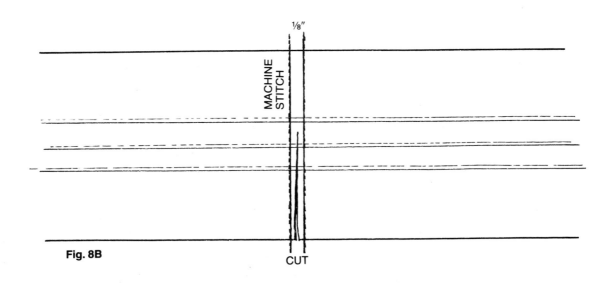

⅛"

MACHINE STITCH

Fig. 8B

CUT

TUCKED BANDS

Pull and cut the required number of fabric strips the depth needed (allowing for tucks) times the width.

NOTE: The depth is down the selvage and the width is between the selvages.

Pull the same number of threads as you want tucks across the width. Be sure to leave at least 3/4 inch of plain fabric on either side of the tucks toward the long raw edge.

French seam the strips together, matching the pulled threads. Make sure the seams are 1/8 inch wide each time.

Fold the fabric on each pulled thread and sew tiny running stitches the desired width from the folded edge.

The distance between the pulled thread and the distance sewn from the folded edge will determine the size the tuck will be. Bring the needle up from the underside of the strip and start at one seam, hiding the knot within the fold. (See Figure 9B.) Try to have enough thread to do at least one section at the time; ;if you do run out of thread, take the thread to the wrong side and knot. Come back up in the same place with a new thread and continue to sew.

Press tucks in the direction you want them to go.

NOTE: With tucks, other than pin tucks, one (1) thread may be pulled to fold on and one (1) thread pulled to sew on, thus insuring straight tucks. (See Figure 5B.)

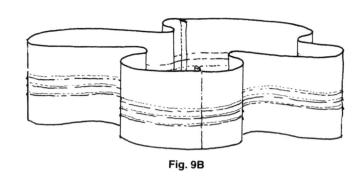

Fig. 9B

Fig. 10B

TUCKED
RUFFLE

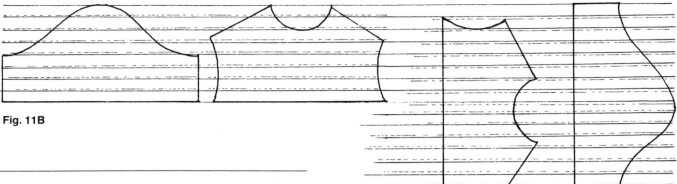

Fig. 11B

TUCKED RUFFLES

Allowing for tucks, pull and cut the number of strips for ruffle depth needed, times (X) the width. (Ruffles are generally one and one-half (1½) to two (2) times the measurement for fulness, depending upon their use.) (See Figure 10B.)

Start measurements for tucks from the bottom edge of the ruffle and never tuck more than 1/3 the depth. Always leave enough fabric on the bottom edge to roll and whip (approximately 3/4 inch).

Matching the pulled threads, French seam the strips to form one large circle. Make seams 1/8 inch wide each time.

Fold on each pulled thread and bring the needle up from the underside, starting at a seam, and sew with tiny running or whipped stitches, depending upon the type of tuck wanted.

Press all tucks toward the bottom of the ruffle.

Roll and whip the bottom edge.

Finish the rolled edge with an appropriate trim. (See Figure 10B.)

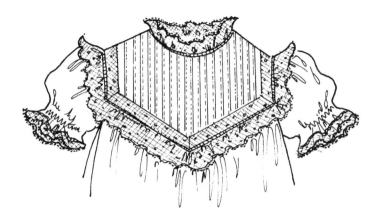

Fig. 11B (Detail)

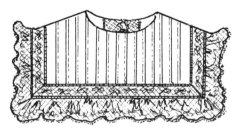

Fig. 11B (Detail)

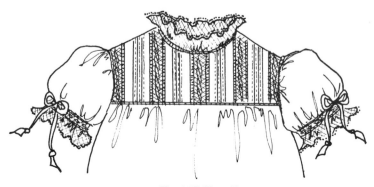

Fig. 11B (Detail)

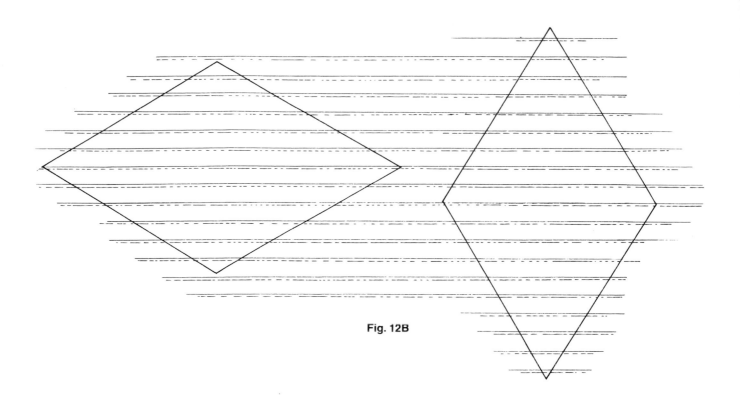

Fig. 12B

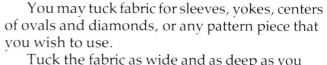

TUCKED FABRIC

You may tuck fabric for sleeves, yokes, centers of ovals and diamonds, or any pattern piece that you wish to use.

Tuck the fabric as wide and as deep as you need. Place the pattern on the tucked strip and draw the outline with a pencil. Machine stitch on the pencil line to keep tucks from coming unsewn. Cut fabric just outside the pencil line. (See Figures 11B, 12B.)

Fig. 12B (Detail)

Fig. 12B (Detail)

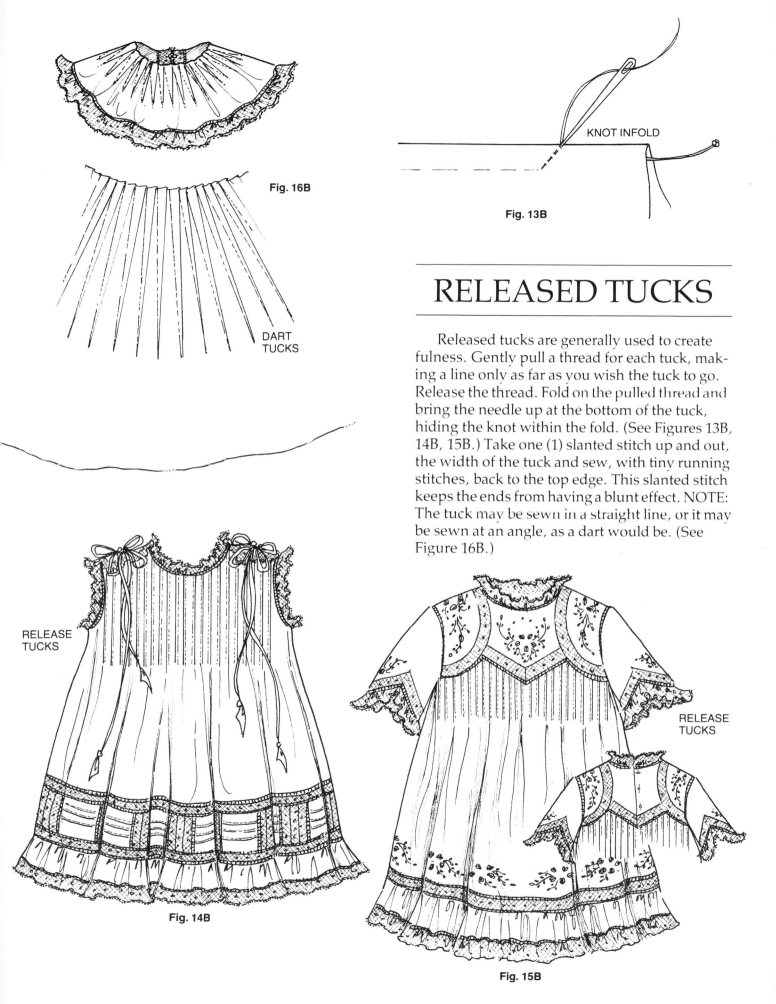

Fig. 16B

DART TUCKS

KNOT INFOLD

Fig. 13B

RELEASED TUCKS

Released tucks are generally used to create fulness. Gently pull a thread for each tuck, making a line only as far as you wish the tuck to go. Release the thread. Fold on the pulled thread and bring the needle up at the bottom of the tuck, hiding the knot within the fold. (See Figures 13B, 14B, 15B.) Take one (1) slanted stitch up and out, the width of the tuck and sew, with tiny running stitches, back to the top edge. This slanted stitch keeps the ends from having a blunt effect. NOTE: The tuck may be sewn in a straight line, or it may be sewn at an angle, as a dart would be. (See Figure 16B.)

RELEASE TUCKS

Fig. 14B

RELEASE TUCKS

Fig. 15B

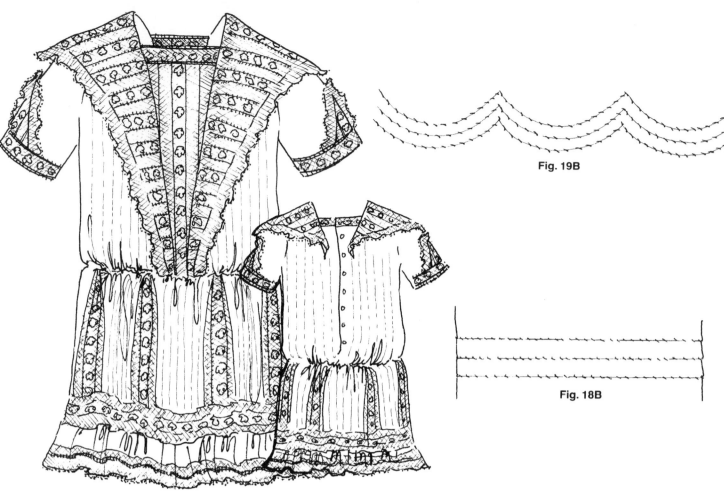

Fig. 19B

Fig. 18B

WHIPPED TUCKS

Prepare band, strip, or ruffle in the same way as for pin tucks, but remember when measuring, that whipped tucks DO NOT TAKE UP THE WIDTH OR DEPTH OF THE FABRIC.

Fold on each pulled thread and sew with a fine whipped stitch (stitches should be about 1/8 inch apart). (See Figures 17B, 18B.)

Scalloped tucks can be made by drawing the design lightly with a pencil and whipping the line. These are very effective when several rows are spaced one over the other and enhanced with tiny sprays of embroidery. (See Figure 19B.)

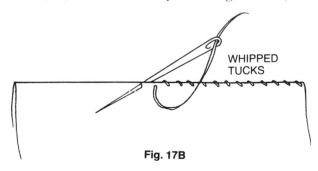

WHIPPED TUCKS

Fig. 17B

WHIPPED TUCKS ON BABY DRESS

PUFFING

I have designed and made many creations through the years, but the one that I treasure most is the wedding train that I designed and made for my three daughters.

The twelve foot train of white Swiss batiste and Valenciennes Lace is detachable and was designed to be worn with each of the three batiste wedding dresses. It is bordered with twenty-five medallions made with puffing and lace and embroidered in white work. Thirteen of the medallions are embroidered with the two designs that were painted on the ceiling of St. Johns Episcopal Church in the 1800's. The designs, painted on hand hewn timber, had been covered with soot from the old stoves that were used to heat the church. They were discovered when the building was undergoing restoration and were restored to their original beauty. The other twelve medallions were designed to record the important events in each daughter's life. Each has four medallions centered with her monogram worked with Old English letters that are encircled with a wreath of flowers and the dates of their birth, baptism, confirmation and marriage.

It is an unusual work of art, made with an abundance of love. I hope that it will be worn and cherished by many generations to come.

PUFFING

Puffing is a technique used in French hand-sewing to achieve softness and fullness in the fabric. It is done by rolling, whipping, and gathering, with equal tension, both sides of a strip of fabric. The result, a soft, shirred strip, can be inserted, either vertically or horizontally, in a yoke, a French Bonnet, or a skirt band.

Puffing strips must always be pulled from selvage to selvage and must be made on a paper guide with the wrong side up. Never take puffing off of the paper until the entredeux or lace has been whipped to both sides.

PUFFING
BANDS

SLIP
DETAIL

PUFFING STRIP

Pull and cut a straight strip of material 1/2 inch wider and two times longer than the puffing strip should be when finished. See Figure 3C. (It might be necessary to French seam two stripes together for length.)

Cut a brown paper guide 1 inch wider and the exact length the puffing strip should be when finished.

Pin the material to the paper at each end with the right side down and the wrong side facing you. See Figure 4C.

Roll and whip and gather each long side of the puffing strip to fit the paper guide. See Figure 5C.

Adjust gathers evenly on both sides so that the folds of the puffing will be straight up and down. Insert pins vertically to secure.

Trim entredeux on one side.

Lay the trimmed side next to the rolled edge of the puffing with the right side down on the paper and whip together by going under the roll and through each entredeux hole. See Figure 6C, 8C and 7C.

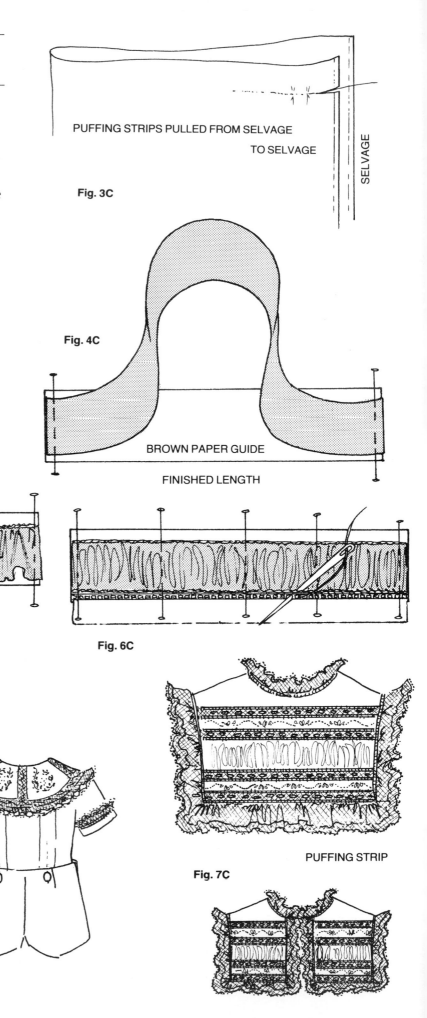

PUFFING STRIPS PULLED FROM SELVAGE

TO SELVAGE

SELVAGE

Fig. 3C

Fig. 4C

BROWN PAPER GUIDE

FINISHED LENGTH

Fig. 5C

Fig. 6C

PUFFING STRIP

Fig. 7C

PUFFING STRIP

Fig. 8C

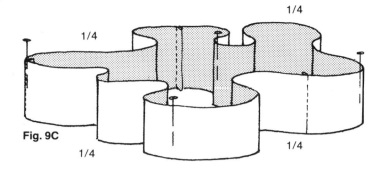

Fig. 9C

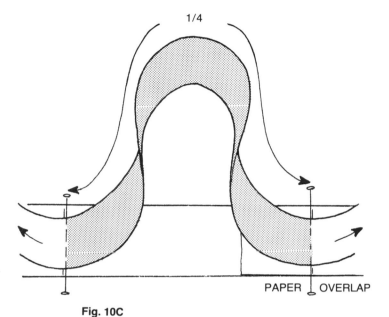

Fig. 10C

PAPER | OVERLAP

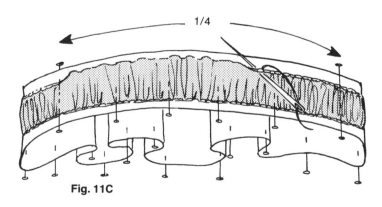

Fig. 11C

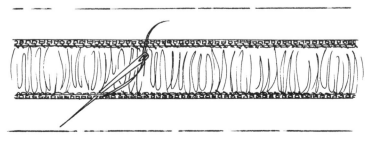

Fig. 12C

PUFFING BAND

Pull and cut strips of material for puffing. The strips should be 1/2 inch wider and two times longer than the finished strip will be.

French seam all of the strips together to form one large circle.

Mark each fourth with a pin or colored thread loop. See Figure 9C.

Cut a strip of heavy brown paper several inches wider and two inches longer than the desired measurement of the puffing strip.

Bring the ends of the paper together and overlap 2 inches. Secure the ends with tape or sew together on the machine.

Put a vertical pencil line at each fourth of the paper guide.

With right sides of the material down and the wrong side facing you, pin 1/4 puffing strip to 1/4 paper guide.

Match pins or thread loops with vertical pencil lines. See Figure 10C.

Roll and whip and gather each 1/4 section of puffing strip to fit a 1/4 section on the paper guide. Adjust gathers evenly and pin securely to paper with pins going vertically. Do one complete side at a time and make sure the gathers are straight up and down. See Figure 11C.

Trim entredeux on one side. Lay the trimmed side next to the rolled edge of the puffing with the right side down on the paper, and whip together by going under the roll and through each entredeux hole.

DO NOT TAKE PUFFING OFF PAPER UNTIL ENTREDEUX IS SEWN TO BOTH SIDES. See Figure 12C.

PUFFING MEDALLION

This type of puffing is made in a circle on a flat surface. The finished length is the same as that of the outer edge of the circle to be covered and the finished width is the distance between the lace insertions. Puffing strips are always cut ½" wider and two times the length of the finished puffing.

Cut a brown paper circle and mark where the lace and puffing are to be. See Figure 14C.

Pull and cut one or more strips of the material the width needed, plus two (2) times the outer measurement.

French seam all the strips, end to end, to form one large circle.

Put a pin or colored thread loop at each fourth. See Figure 15C.

Mark the paper pattern in fourths with a pencil line.

Pin 1/4 of the puffing to a 1/4 section of the pattern, matching pins or thread loops to the pencil lines. See Figure 16C.

Roll and whip and gather the outer edge in

BROWN PAPER CIRCLE

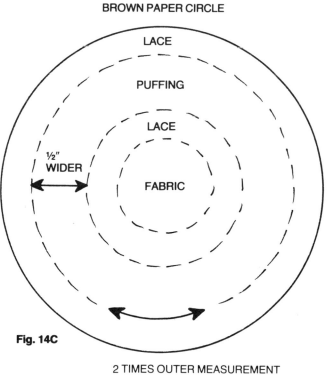

Fig. 14C

2 TIMES OUTER MEASUREMENT

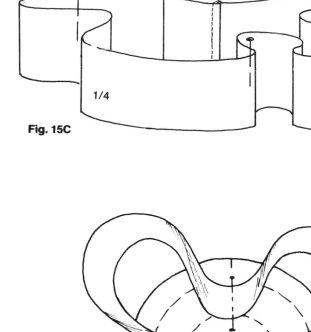

Fig. 15C

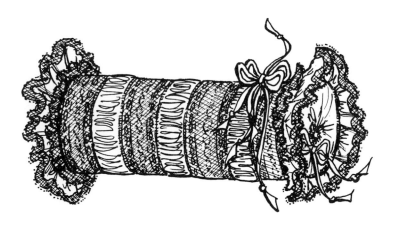

PENCIL LINES

Fig. 16C

equal fourths to fit the paper. Pin to secure.

Roll the inner edge to fit the paper. Pin to secure. See Figure 17C. NOTE: The gathers cannot be straight across, but be sure to even them on the curve so that they will lie nicely.

Trim the material off one side of the entredeux and clip the material on the other side so that it will turn easily. See Figure 18C.

Pin the trimmed side, right side down, to the curved edge of the puffing, making sure that it is full enough not to pucker. Whip together side by side.

Trim the other side of the entredeux.

Baste lace insertion, right side down, to the paper next to the puffing, on each side. Whip the lace to the entredeux on the puffing. See Figure 19C.

Take the medallion off the paper. Lay it on the material to which it is to be applied and tiny baste the outer edge.

Use the buttonhole stitch to apply the outer edges of the lace to the fabric. After buttonholing is completed, trim the material from behind the medallion, within 1/8 inch of the lace insertion. This leaves a fabric center to be embroidered, if desired. See Figure 20C.

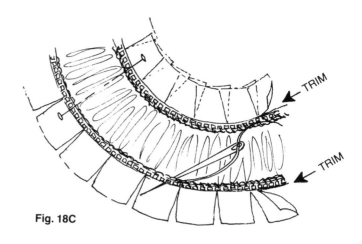

Fig. 18C

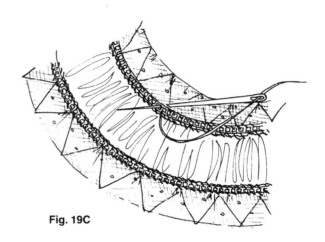

Fig. 19C

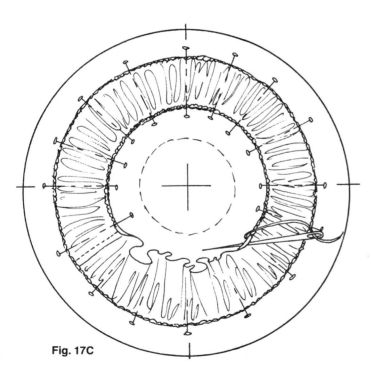

Fig. 17C

Fig. 20C

HEIRLOOM
CREATIONS
from
Sarah Howard Stone

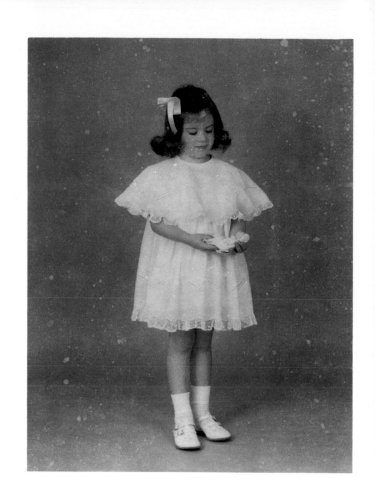

PUFFING FOR BERTHA COLLARS OR ROUND YOKES

Puffing for a collar or yoke is worked similarly to puffing for a medallion in that the top or inside is not gathered equally to the bottom or outside, but is different because it is worked in one long strip rather than a strip which has been joined into a circle.

The use of puffing and lace permits numerous designs for Bertha collars and round yokes. The number of rows and the spacing of the lace determines the width and number of rows of puffing needed.

Entredeux may be used between the puffing and lace in a yoke, but not in a collar because it will make a collar too stiff. See Figures 21C & 22C.

Cut the collar or yoke pattern out of brown paper. Put the lace on the paper as desired, creating design. (Remember that when working with the paper, the right side of the fabric or lace is down and the wrong side is facing up.) Pull and cut strip(s) for puffing. See Figure 23C.
NOTE: Fabric strips must be pulled from selvage to selvage and must be two times the bottom measurement of each puffing strip and 1/2 inch wider than the space between the lace.

Roll and whip and gather the top of the puffing strip in equal halves and fit under the lace insertion. Pin securely with pins going vertically. See Figure 24C.

Roll and whip and gather the bottom of the puffing strip to fit the paper.
NOTE: This is one time that the gathers cannot be straight across, but be sure to even them on the curve so that they lie nicely.

For collars, where entredeux is not used, whip the lace and puffing together by going under the roll and through the heavy line of the lace with stitches 1/8 inch apart. See Figure 22C.

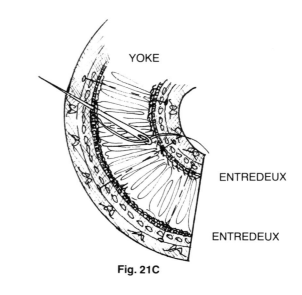

YOKE

ENTREDEUX

ENTREDEUX

Fig. 21C

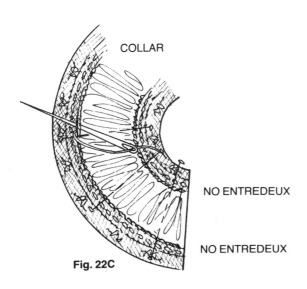

COLLAR

NO ENTREDEUX

NO ENTREDEUX

Fig. 22C

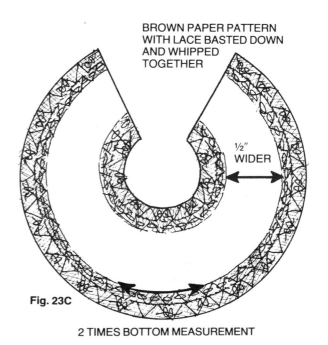

BROWN PAPER PATTERN WITH LACE BASTED DOWN AND WHIPPED TOGETHER

½" WIDER

Fig. 23C

2 TIMES BOTTOM MEASUREMENT

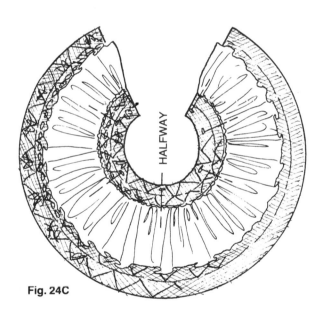

Fig. 24C

ROUND YOKE

Fig. 25C

BERTHA COLLAR

Fig. 26C

66

LACE& LACE WORK

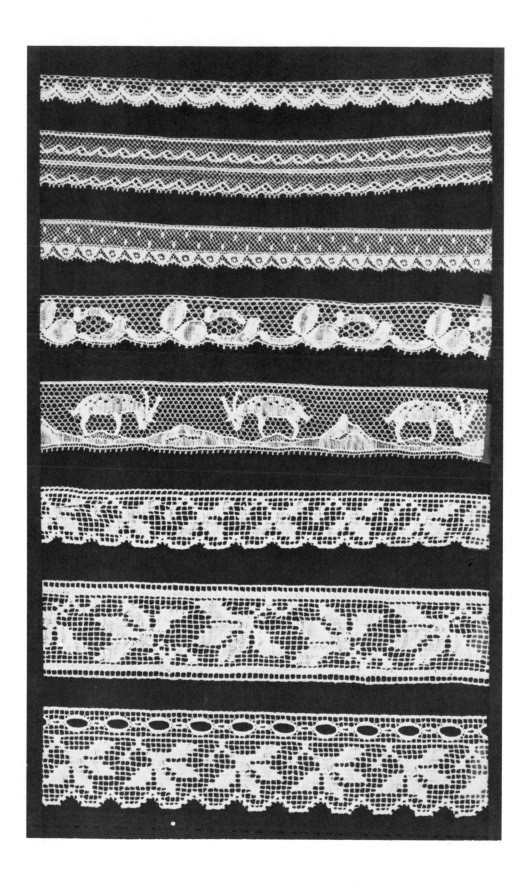

LACE

A Brief History of Machine-made Lace[1]

Numerous books have been written about handmade lace, and the lace itself can be seen in museum exhibits throughout the world. However, there is little known about the lace that we use in handsewing today, and I thought that my readers might be interested in knowing more about the history of lace and how lace is made.

The lace machine was developed in England and had progressed, by 1780, from the early stocking frame to the net machine. In 1802, Robert Brown developed an excellent machine that produced net of all sizes to be used as background on which to work designs by hand. Improvements on the machines continued and, in 1809, Heathcoat obtained a patent for a "bobbin net" machine. This opened the way for John Ieavers who, in 1813, worked out the principles of this machine that produced a fancy pattern at the same time the net was being formed. This machine-produced lace was very close in appearance and quality to handmade lace.

The English patents on the machines expired in 1826, but even before that date, many machines had already been disassembled and smuggled into France. While Nottingham, England was the birthplace of machine-made lace and does still enjoy a large distribution of lace and great prestige throughout the world, most of the lace that we use today comes from Calais, France.

It was inevitable that Calais would become the center of the lace industry in France. Not only was Calais located close to Paris where fashion was affluent, but many English immigrants settled there during the period from 1348 to 1558.

The last major improvement to the Ieavers machine, a punch-card system known as the Jacquad control system, was also achieved by France, in 1837. It allowed the most intricate handmade patterns to be reproduced by machine, achieving beauty and quality almost equal to that of hand crafted lace.

Today, visitors to Calais are surprised by the tremendous size of the lace machine. It weighs seventeen tons and covers a 10 x 50 square foot area of floor space. It is truly amazing that this monstrosity is capable of producing lace of such beauty and delicacy.

Valencinne, the lace we use most in handsewing, was the lace mainly produced until the demands from the fashion world brought about the advanced technology and skill to reproduce other types of lace such as Chantilly, Binche, Alencon, and Point de Paris.

Because of their love of lace and their desire to maintain the quality and beauty of the handmade lace, the old lace makers became the life line of the new process. Their skill and artistry has survived through their descendants.

Perfections to the machine made lace did not come overnight. Even though lace was produced on the machine, there were numerous processes such as washing, clipping, cutting, and dying that had to be performed by hand. One by one these processes have been mechanized; however, even today, with all the mechanical devices in use, the making of lace still requires the human touch and the expertise of artists and technicians.

In the earlier years of machine-made lace, the predominate fibers used were the same fibers as those used for handmade lace, cotton and silk. In recent years, man made fibers, rayon and nylon, have been added to the natural fiber, enabling the production of old patterns of lace made from blends that go well with our modern day world of wash and wear.

[1]David E. Schwab, *The Story of Lace and Embroidery and Handkerchiefs*, (New York: Fairchild Publications, 1957), pp. 38-42.

LACES USED IN FRENCH HANDSEWING[2]

Baby Irish — A lace made by hand in widths up to four inches. It originated in Ireland and is distinguished by its crocheted characteristics.

Baby Lace — A descriptive term used for very light, narrow laces, generally Valenciennes, Cluny, or Crochet.

Binche Lace — Originally hand made in the town of Hainault in Flanders, Binche lace is made of cotton and is easily recognizable by its fancy net. It belongs to the Valenciennes family and is used in the same manner. Reproductions by machine are produced in England, France and the United States.

[2]Ibid., pp. 60-64.

Cluny Lace — A course, strong lace still made by hand in LePuy, France, Belgium and China. It was formerly made of linen but is now made from cotton. Its name was taken from the Cluny Museum in Paris, France. Imitations are produced on machine.

Filet Lace — Square meshes with the squares partially filled in to form a design.

Maline Lace — Originally made by hand in Maline, Belgium, this lace is now made by machine in Calais and Caudry, France and Nottingham, England. It is characterized by small pretty floral designs on fine net ground.

Picot Lace — A finishing lace of narrow loops, round or triangular shaped.

Valenciennes Laces ("Vals") — This lace, first made by hand and later by machine in Valenciennes, France, is the best known and most widely used in French handsewing. The ground net which today is made of cotton, nylon, or a combination of the two, has round or square holes and a flat sheer design. These designs include simple flowers, dots and a scalloped edge.

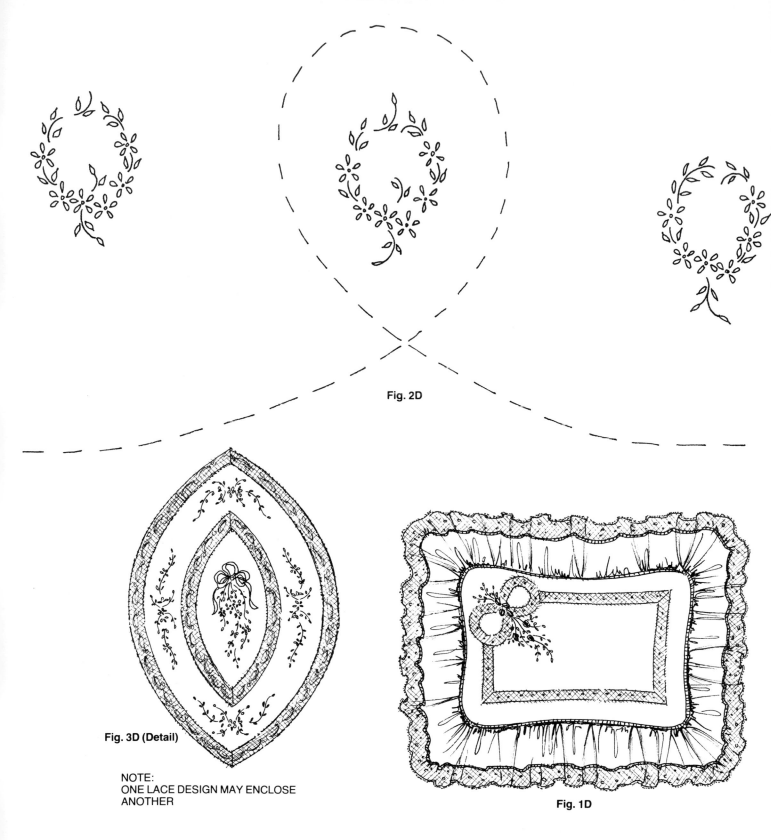

Fig. 2D

Fig. 3D (Detail)

NOTE:
ONE LACE DESIGN MAY ENCLOSE
ANOTHER

Fig. 1D

LACEWORK

Lace may be applied to fabric in many shapes, creating very beautiful and pleasing effects. See Figure 1D. Lace designs are further enhanced by embroidery, tucks, or puffing. See Figure 2D. The lace may form a design in a skirt, see Figure 3D, or it may be used as the bottom edge of the skirt. See Figure 4D. I have included several patterns for ovals, diamonds, and teardrops to be used on collars and skirts. They may be joined by scallops that can be drawn using a saucer or plate as a guide. Do not cut the bottom edge of a skirt before applying the lace. Draw a collar on a square of fabric and complete the lace work before trimming the fabric away.

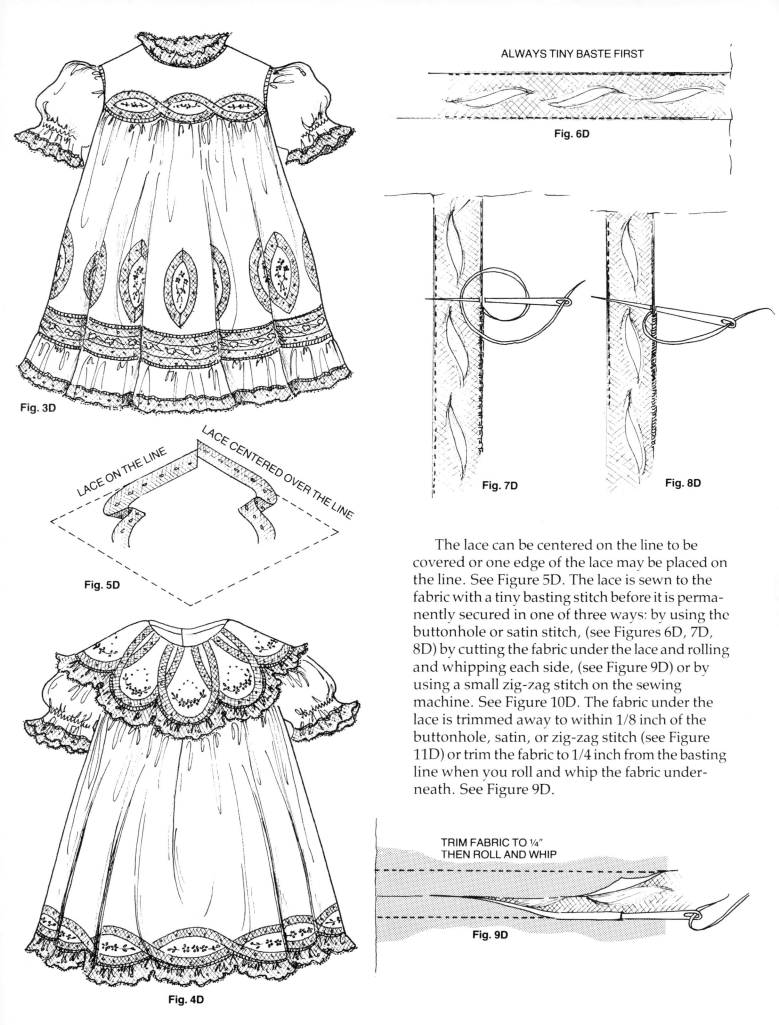

Fig. 3D

LACE ON THE LINE

LACE CENTERED OVER THE LINE

Fig. 5D

Fig. 4D

ALWAYS TINY BASTE FIRST

Fig. 6D

Fig. 7D

Fig. 8D

The lace can be centered on the line to be covered or one edge of the lace may be placed on the line. See Figure 5D. The lace is sewn to the fabric with a tiny basting stitch before it is permanently secured in one of three ways: by using the buttonhole or satin stitch, (see Figures 6D, 7D, 8D) by cutting the fabric under the lace and rolling and whipping each side, (see Figure 9D) or by using a small zig-zag stitch on the sewing machine. See Figure 10D. The fabric under the lace is trimmed away to within 1/8 inch of the buttonhole, satin, or zig-zag stitch (see Figure 11D) or trim the fabric to 1/4 inch from the basting line when you roll and whip the fabric underneath. See Figure 9D.

TRIM FABRIC TO ¼"
THEN ROLL AND WHIP

Fig. 9D

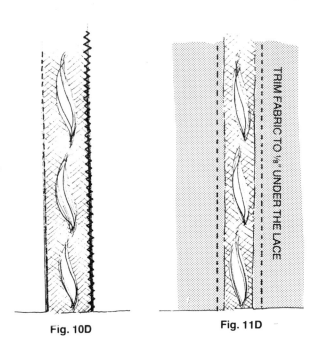

Fig. 10D

Fig. 11D

TRIM FABRIC TO ⅛" UNDER THE LACE

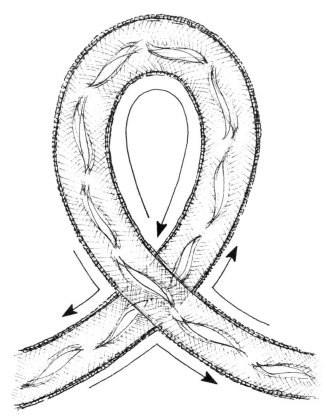

Fig. 12D

Do not sew the lace to the fabric at the point where it crosses. See Figure 12D. The lace is sewn together after the fabric has been cut away. (See Figures 13D, 14D and 15D.)

FABRIC CUT AWAY UNDER THE LACE

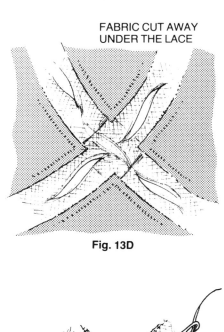

Fig. 13D

Fig. 15D

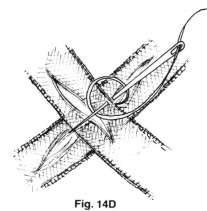

Fig. 14D

DETAIL OF LACE ON COLLAR

TUCK RAW EDGE OF LACE UNDER
TINY BASTE THEN BUTTONHOLE

Fig. 16D

LACE COLLAR & TABS ARE
MADE AND THEN ATTACHED
TO THE DRESS AT THE NECK AND
BOTTOM OF THE TABS

Fig. 18D

EXAMPLES OF LACE WORK

Fig. 17D

INSTRUCTIONS TO CREATE
LACE MOTIFS

1. Transfer the design to the fabric with a #2 lead pencil.
2. Lay the lace behind the basket motif.
3. Tiny baste the fabric to the lace from the right side of the fabric on the pencil line.
4. Buttonhole or satin stitch over the basting thread.
5. Trim the fabric close to the buttonhole or satin stitch exposing the lace.
6. Trim the raw edges of the lace underneath the fabric close to the stitching line.

Any design that you choose may be worked in like manner.

LACE
BASKETS

Fig. 19D

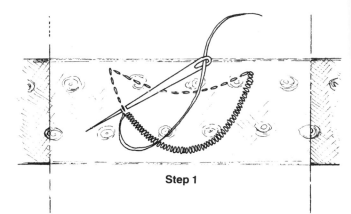

Step 1

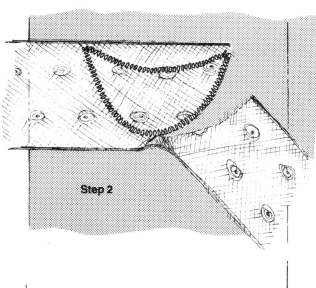

Step 2

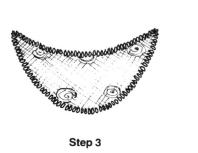

Step 3

CREATE
YOUR OWN
LACE DESIGN

Fig. 20D

NOTE: TRIANGLE APPEARS 8 TIMES ON SKIRT

LACE BUTTERLY

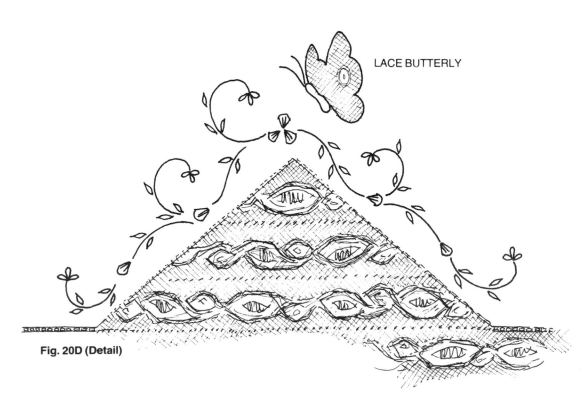

Fig. 20D (Detail)

PATTERN
REPEATS
HERE

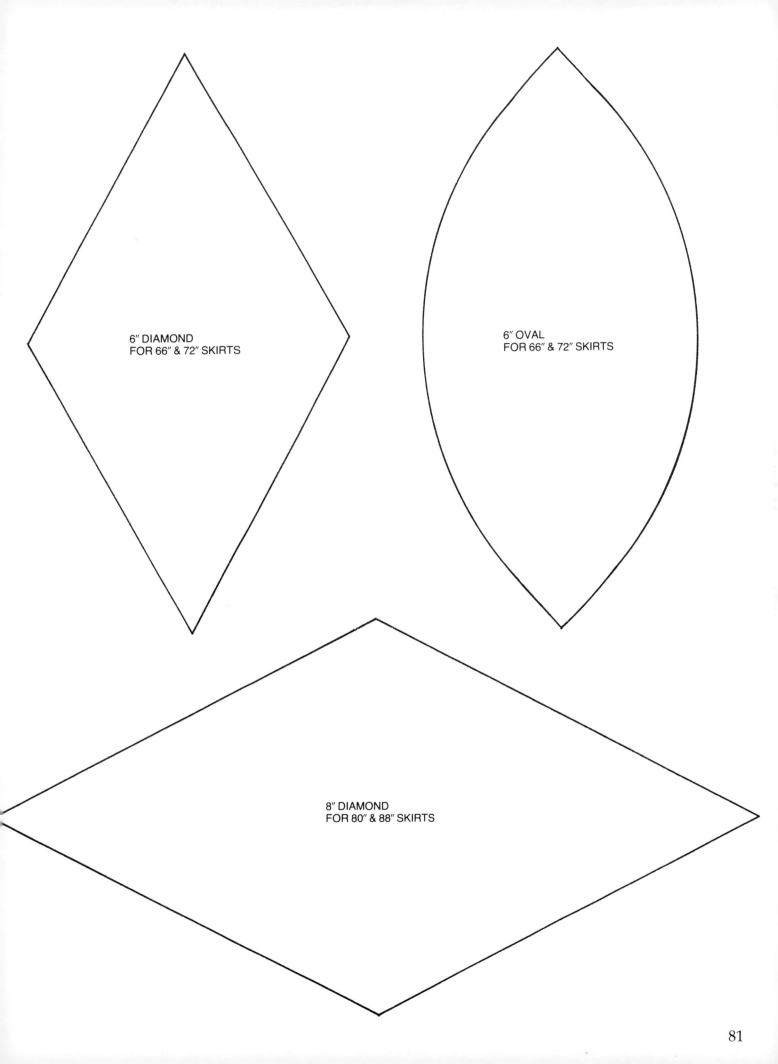

6″ DIAMOND
FOR 66″ & 72″ SKIRTS

6″ OVAL
FOR 66″ & 72″ SKIRTS

8″ DIAMOND
FOR 80″ & 88″ SKIRTS

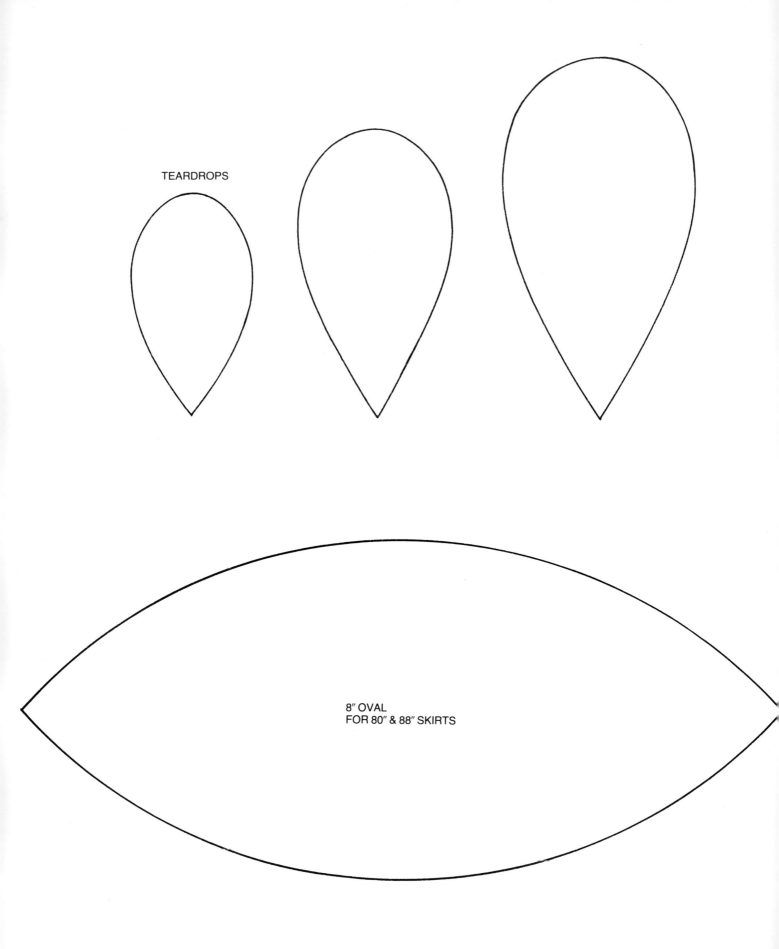

TEARDROPS

8" OVAL
FOR 80" & 88" SKIRTS

Bibliography
Schwab, David E. *The Story of Lace and Embroidery and Handkerchiefs*.
New York: Fairchild Publications, 1957.

EMBROIDERY

EMBROIDERY

Evidence of early embroidery, dating back to the 8th century, has been found on fragments of cloth and leather, and depicted on primitive sculptures and paintings. The embroidery was used then as it is now, for pure decoration and not for utility.

Later, embroidery was extensively used for religious purposes and, in the 13th century in England, beautiful church vestments were embroidered with a special couching stitch that completely covered the material.

Under the reign of Henry VIII came the English Reformation and the disappearance of the Church influence in the arts. The chief teachers of arts and crafts, the monks and nuns, were banished. For a time, under both Henry VIII and his daughter Elizabeth, all arts suffered severely in England. When embroidery was taken up again, it was used principally for household adornment, and became more and more lavish.

History books repeatedly depict women of all walks of life, from queens to commoners, embroidering a variety of things for a variety of reasons. The more affluent families often hired servants because of their skills in sewing and embroidery.

Though there are many types and classifications of embroidery, we are primarily interested in White Work, which simply means white embroidery on white material. White Work reached its peak during the Victorian era when the simple stitches on "sewn muslin" were replaced by Venetian, French, or Ayrshire Embroidery. It was during this time that White Work became popular in America when feather stitch, satin stitch, stem stitch and french knots were much in evidence, as they still are today.

The designs that I have created for this book will be excellent for White Work, and will be equally as beautiful when worked in pastels.

As fashions change, so do materials, but throughout the years, it has been a fast rule that dainty stitches are more effective on fine transparent materials such as handkerchief linen, batiste, lawn, organdy, fine silks, and wool challis.

It is possible to transfer most designs directly to the material by lightly tracing the motif with a #2 lead pencil. (NOTE: Trace the motifs from this book to tissue paper or onion paper and then lay the material over the paper and pin it securely before transferring.) The embroidery thread us-ually covers the pencil lines, but what marks are left uncovered will wash out very nicely. If the fabric is too heavy to see through, trace the motif on tissue or onion paper and then transfer it to the material, using dressmakers' carbon paper. (NOTE: Place the carbon paper face down between the material and the design.) A more defined motif will be achieved by placing all three thicknesses (motif, carbon paper, and fabric) on a flat, hard surface and using a fine hard pencil to trace.

It is advisable to embroider the design on the fabric before cutting it out. (NOTE: Trace the pattern piece and the embroidery on a square of material. REMEMBER: DO NOT CUT OUT.) Hand baste the outline of the pattern (such as a yoke, a collar, etc.) (See Figure 1E.) with a pastel sewing thread, complete the embroidery, wash, and then iron, with right side down, on a thick terry towel. This will leave the embroidery with a raised effect. Now cut out.

It is important to pull threads and cut strips of material for skirts or bands and French seam them into a circle before transferring the design onto them. Roll and whip the raw edges of the band or the bottom of the skirt before working the embroidery. Wash and iron all work before applying entredeux and lace.

The starting point of a stitch should not be visible. Use a small knot only when the back of the work will be concealed; otherwise, start by taking several running stitches toward the starting point and then making a small backstitch. To end the thread, take a small backstitch or run the thread in and out through the embroidery on the wrong side.

It is always advisable to have a separate box or basket for your embroidery tools and supplies. I would suggest that you purchase a small hoop, ten (size 10) and twelve (12) crewel needles, a 3" pair of embroidery scissors, a stiletto for making eyelets, heavy paper for faggoting, tissue paper, dressmaker's carbon paper, and a good pencil for transferring designs. Complete your basket with a supply of high quality, six-strand cotton floss and pearl cotton thread, and maybe a thimble for the middle finger if you like.

The embroidery stitches that are explained in this book are nothing more than variations of the flat, the knotted, the linked (or chained), and the looped (or blanket) stitch.

To become an artist with needle and thread requires only that one have a love of beauty and a sense of perfection.

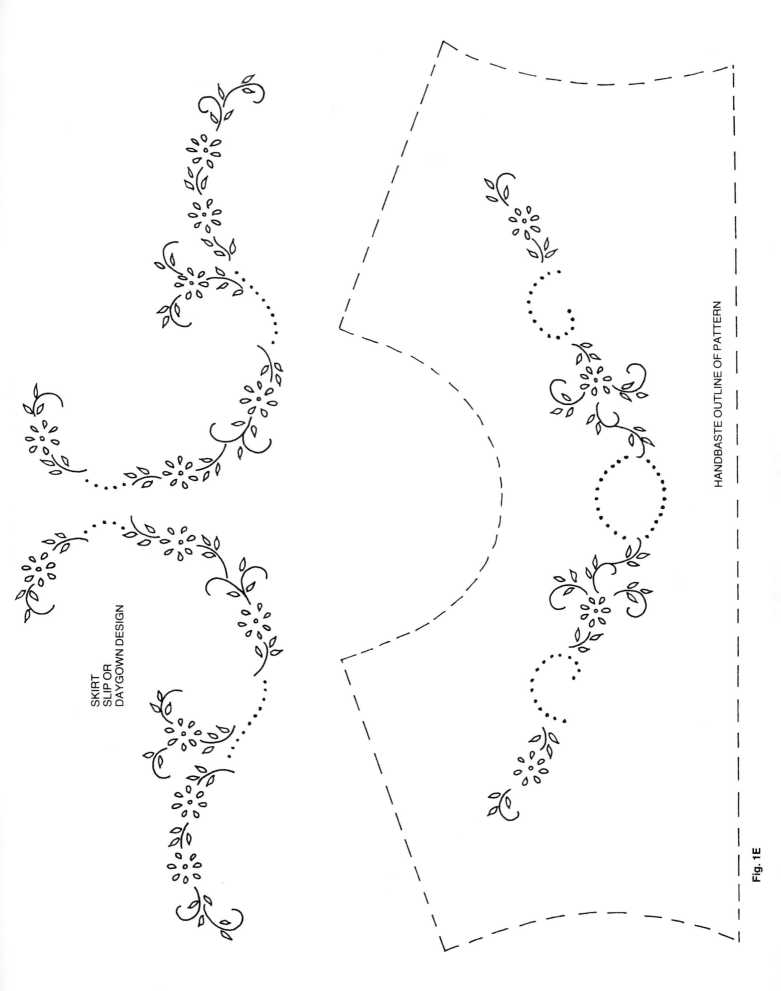

SKIRT
SLIP OR
DAYGOWN DESIGN

HANDBASTE OUTLINE OF PATTERN

Fig. 1E

87

Any of the embroidery designs in this book may be worked in a variety of stitches. These are the stitches most commonly used.

A. Flower Centers — French Knits, Eyelet, or Satin Stitch
B. Flower Petals — Satin Stitch or Lazy Daisy
C. Leaves — Satin Stitch, Lazy Daisy, or Bullion
D. Stems — Outline or Stem Stitch
E. Rose — Satin Stitch with Eyelet Center
F. Bullion Rose — Bullion Rose Stitch
G. French Knot Flower — French Knot or Mock French Knot

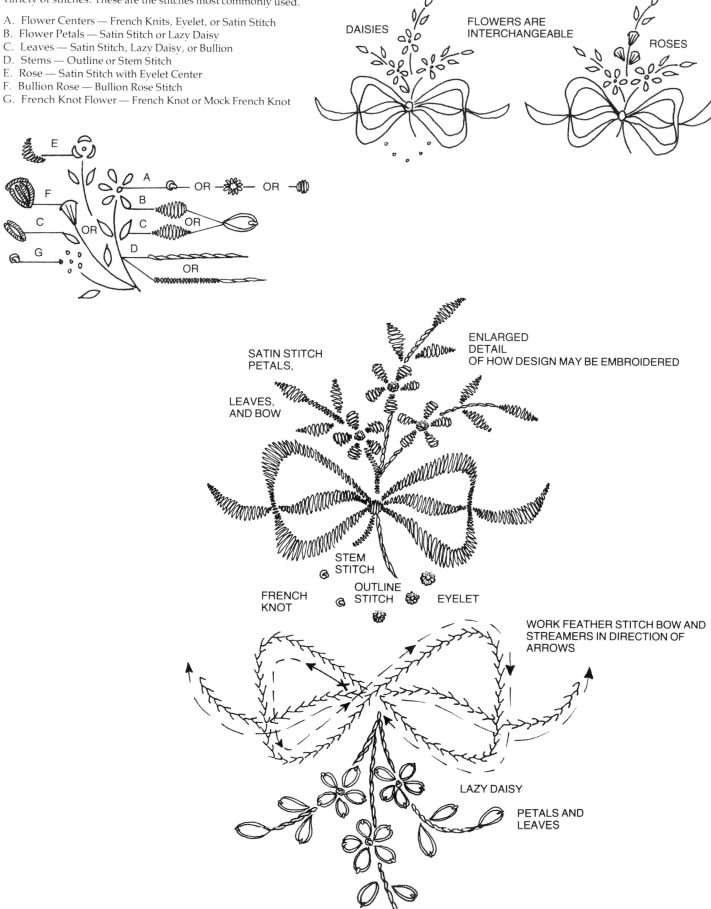

DAISIES   FLOWERS ARE INTERCHANGEABLE   ROSES

SATIN STITCH PETALS,

LEAVES, AND BOW

ENLARGED DETAIL OF HOW DESIGN MAY BE EMBROIDERED

STEM STITCH

FRENCH KNOT

OUTLINE STITCH   EYELET

WORK FEATHER STITCH BOW AND STREAMERS IN DIRECTION OF ARROWS

LAZY DAISY

PETALS AND LEAVES

BACK STITCH

This stitch may be used in sewing, as well as in embroidery. It is used for lines and outlines; therefore, it is very important that each stitch be even in size and placement.

Always start at the right end of the line bringing the needle to the right side of the material, a stitch length from point A. Insert the needle at B and come up at C, picking up twice the amount of material as covered by the first stitch. (See Figure 2E.)

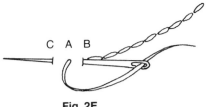

Fig. 2E

BUD STITCH

Work two satin stitched lines to form a V (usually the end of a stem). Work the bud with a single thread. Start with the center stitch and work two (2) more stitches on either side, taking shorter stitches as you go out from center. (See Figure 3E.)

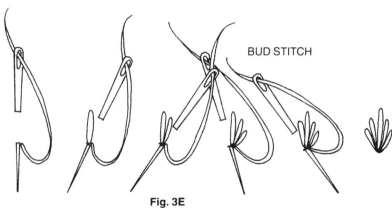

BUD STITCH

Fig. 3E

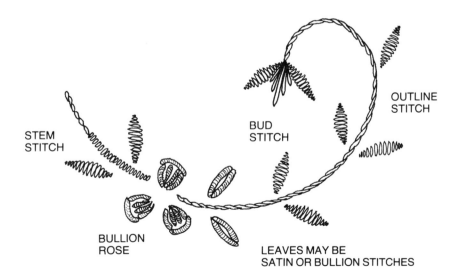

STEM STITCH

BUD STITCH

OUTLINE STITCH

BULLION ROSE

LEAVES MAY BE SATIN OR BULLION STITCHES

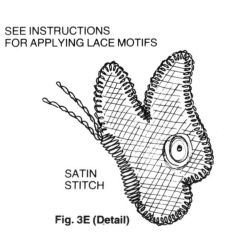

SEE INSTRUCTIONS FOR APPLYING LACE MOTIFS

SATIN STITCH

Fig. 3E (Detail)

BULLION STITCH

This stitch resembles a raised roll of twisted thread lying on the surface of the material; it is also called "roll picot stitch." It is effectively employed to represent veining of leaves, to work entire leaves and flower petals (as well as roses), and may be generally used whenever a raised ornament stitch is desired.

Bring the needle and thread up to the front of the material, (See Figure 4E) put the needle in the material in the position you wish the bullion stitch to be, take as much material on the needle as needed for desired stitch length, and bring the point well out where the thread already is. (See Figure 5E.)

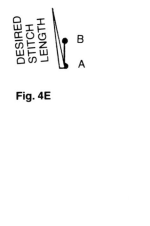

Fig. 4E

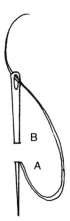

Fig. 5E

With the needle in this position, wind the thread the required number of wraps around the point of the needle with right hand. Ease the thread smoothly and not too tightly toward the eye end of the needle. (See Figures 6E and 7E.)

Keep the twist from falling off the needle by the pressure of the left thumb. Gently pull the needle through the material and through the twist of thread. (See Figure 8E.)

Turn the thread towards the top of the stitch and pull until the stitch lies in position with the twisted thread in a close roll upon it. (See Figures 9E and 10E.)

Insert the needle again at the top of the bullion stitch and bring it up where the next stitch is to begin. (See Figures 11E and 12E.)

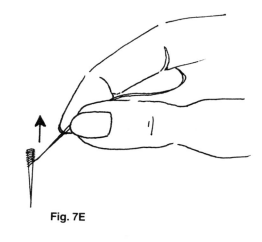

Fig. 7E

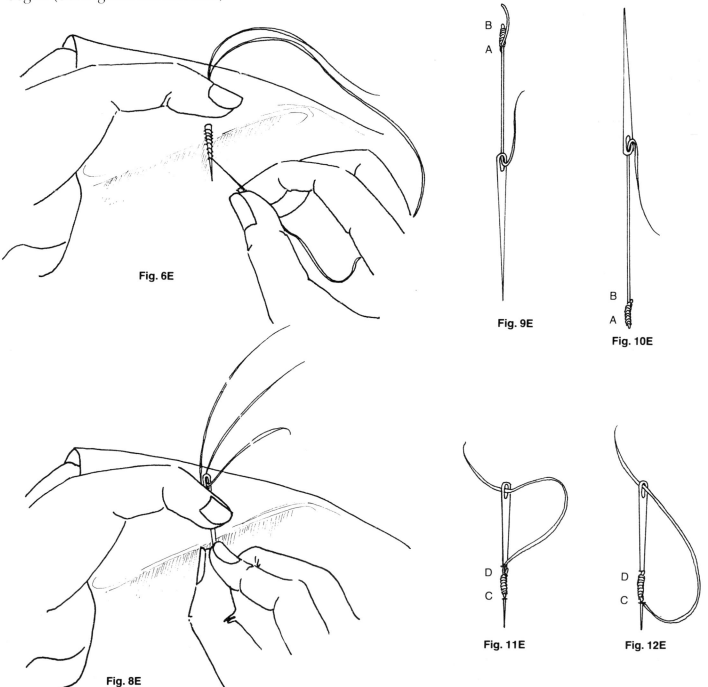

Fig. 6E

Fig. 9E

Fig. 10E

Fig. 11E

Fig. 12E

Fig. 8E

BULLION ROSE

"Handkerchief" or "French" roses, as they are sometimes called, are made with a bullion stitch. The inside of the rose is a shade darker than the outside. They are made with one (1) strand of embroidery thread. The length of the stitch and the number of times that the thread is wrapped around the needle determines the size of the rose.

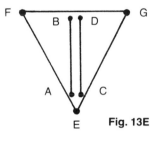

Fig. 13E

ROSE (See Figure 13E.)

AB,CD dark thread	6 wraps each
EF,EG light thread	11 wraps each
FG light thread	13 wraps each

ROSEBUD FOR EMBROIDERY OR SMOCKING (See Figure 14E.)

AB,CD dark thread	8 wraps each
EF above & below light thread	13 wraps each

NOTE: The rosebud is worked over four (4) pleats for smocking. (See Figure 15E.) The rosebud may be accented on either side with a Lazy Daisy leaf worked with two (2) strands of thread. (See Figure 16E.)

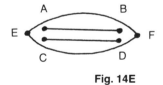

Fig. 14E

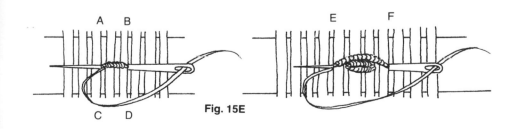

Fig. 15E

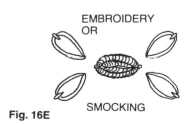

EMBROIDERY OR

SMOCKING

Fig. 16E

CHAIN STITCH

This stitch is used to define design lines or borders. It may also be used as a filling and padding stitch for a raised effect. (See Figure 17E.)

Bring the needle to the right side of the material at A. Form a loop and secure with the left thumb while inserting the needle again at A, and bringing it up at B. (See Figure 18E.) Draw the thread through the loop, being careful not to pull thread too tight. The repeat stitch is made by inserting the needle inside the loop at B. (See Figure 19E.) It is important that stitches be equal in size.

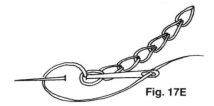

Fig. 17E

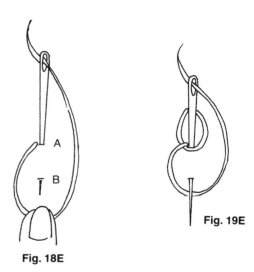

Fig. 18E

Fig. 19E

DOUBLE CORAL STITCH

The beauty of the double coral stitch depends upon its perfect regularity. A novice might want to draw two (2) perpendicular lines about 1/4 inch apart as a guide to ensure evenness. After perfecting the stitch, you may work with just one (1) line.

Bring the needle and thread up at the starting point and, holding the thread under the left hand thumb, make a straight stitch on the right hand side of the line. Bringing the needle over the thread held by the thumbs, draw up. Make another stitch on the same side.

Again, hold the thread under the thumb and make a straight stitch on the line to the left, bringing the needle up over the thread held by the thumb. Make a second stitch on the left side and continue working two (2) stitches alternately on each side. (See Figure 20E.) NOTE: The top of a new stitch must always be level with the bottom of the stitch last worked and the thread must not be drawn too tightly. It is adviseable to work as close to the line as possible.

Fig. 20E

EYELET HOLE

EYELET
TOP SIDE
1. NEEDLE
FROM UNDER SIDE

*UNDERNEATH
2. CATCH LOOSE END
AS YOU WORK EYELET

Eyelets are used as the centers for flowers and to accent embroidery designs. The eyelets used for the motifs in this book are very small and fine; therefore, they do not require a basting stitch around them before working.

Pierce the material with a sewing stiletto or awl. Do it gently so the threads will not be broken.

Using one (1) strand of fine embroidery thread, bring the needle through the material close to the hole, leaving a tail of thread which will be caught as you work closely placed overcasting stitches over the edge. (See Figure 21E and 22E.) It is important not to take up more than one (1) or two (2) threads when overcasting. (See Figure 23E.)

Pull the stitches tightly in order to open up the material. When you complete the circle, take the thread to the wrong side (as shown in Figure 24E) and run the needle under the stitching and clip. (See Figure 25E.)

Fig. 21E

Fig. 22E

Fig. 24E

Fig. 23E

Fig. 25E

FAGGOTING

Faggoting, usually employed for joining two edges, consists of buttonhole stitches taken first on one edge, and then on the other, letting the work progress in the direction of the sewer. When two bands are faggoted together, they are first basted or chain stitched on stiff paper, and then the stitches are added. (See Figures 26 and 27E.) Fasten thread in lower edge of material. Throw thread to left and take small stitch downward in upper edge of material. (See Figure 28E.) Cross diagonally over and take upward stitch in the lower edge of the material (See Figure 29E.) Be sure to always throw thread to left. The illustration clearly shows how the work is done.

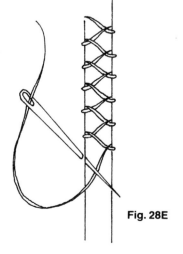

Fig. 29E

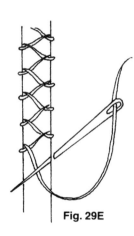

Fig. 28E

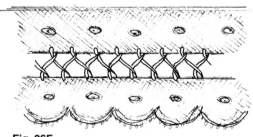

Fig. 26E

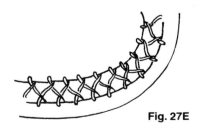

Fig. 27E

FAGOTING MAY BE USED BETWEEN LACE OR BETWEEN BIAS STRIP AND ROUND COLLAR.

FEATHER STITCH

SINGLE — The important point of the single feather stitch is that it should be worked evenly, which will require practice. Once perfected, this stitch is very effective on infant apparel. The smaller the stitch, the more attractive the finished design will be. Trace the design line on the material as a guide for the center of the feather stitching. Bring the needle and thread up on the line at the starting point. Hold the thread under the left thumb and insert the needle in a slanting direction on the right hand side, taking up about 1/8 inch of material. Bring the needle up just below the last stitch, with the point of the needle going over the thread, and draw through. Again, hold the thread under the thumb, turn the needle completely around towards the left, and take a similar stitch slanting to the center. Bring the needle over the thread held by the thumb and draw through. Proceed thus, making the stitches radiate alternately right and left for the length desired. (See Figures 30E and 31E.)

DOUBLE — The double feather stitch is so called because two stitches are worked, one underneath the other, forming double branching lines on each side. The needle is always placed in the material at a slant, as shown in the diagram. Double feather stitch is employed for small feathery sprays, bows, and borders. (See Figure 32E.)

TRIPLE — The triple feather stitch is another variety of this pretty stitch in which three stitches are worked successively on each side of the line. (See Figure 33E.)

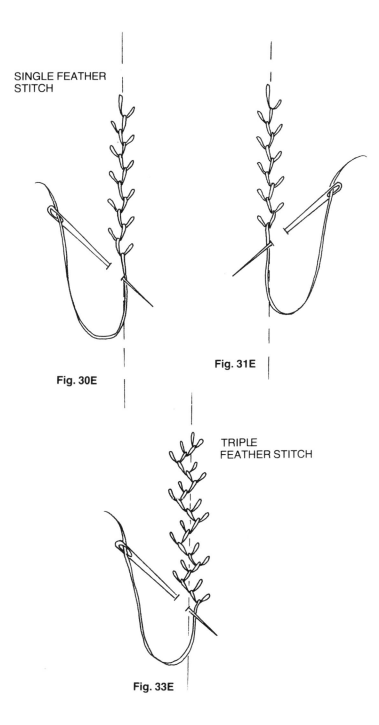

SINGLE FEATHER STITCH

Fig. 30E

Fig. 31E

TRIPLE FEATHER STITCH

Fig. 33E

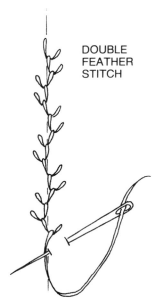

DOUBLE FEATHER STITCH

Fig. 32E

EMBROIDERY DESIGN FOR BAND OF CHALLIS BONNET AND COAT COLLAR

COLLAR

EMBROIDERED BAND AND COLLAR ON
CHALLIS BONNET AND COAT

FRENCH KNOTS

Fig. 34E

A discussion of French embroidery would not be complete without mention of the French Knot, and yet we no longer do that stitch in the French way, which was quite a complicated affair of twists and turnings. For today's French handsewing in delicate white work, the knot is made with one (1) strand of fine embroidery thread. From one (1) to four (4) loops can be made on the needle, depending upon the size of the knot desired. French knots may be used in clusters to form flowers or singular to form the center of a flower.

Fig. 35E

To form the French knots, secure the thread with a small back stitch and draw the thread through the material where the knot is to be completed. With your right hand, lay the needle across the thread, loop the thread around the point of the needle one to four times, hold the loops secure with your thumb and place the needle point as close as possible to where the thread originally came through, drawing the needle and thread all the way through the material. (See Figures 34E and 35E.)

EMBROIDERED DAYGOWN

EMBROIDERY DESIGNED FOR DAYGOWN SKIRT

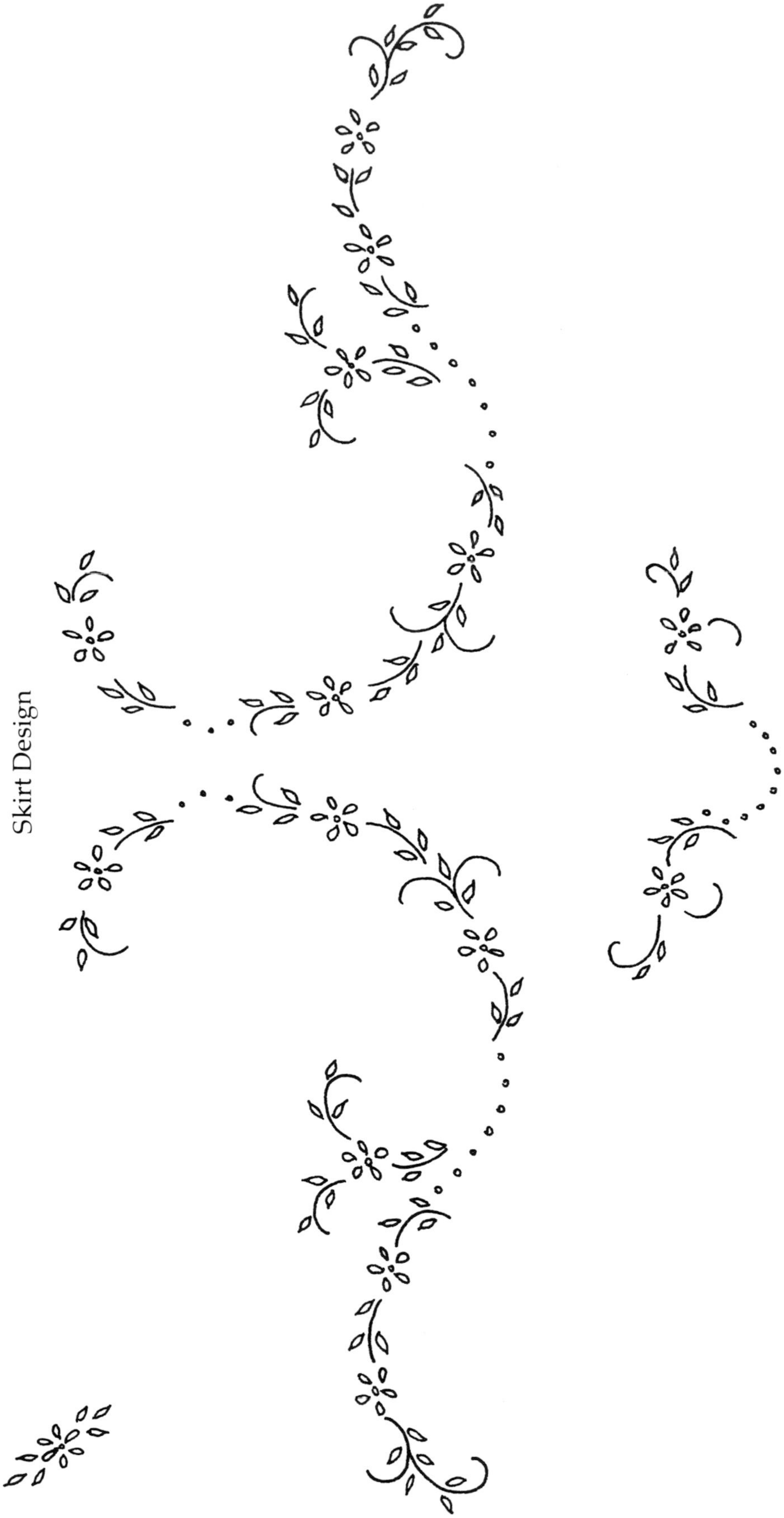

Skirt Design

MOCK FRENCH KNOT

This stitch is made with very little effort and yet is as effective as the more complicated French knot. It is worked with a double thread.

Bring the needle and thread through the material and, wrapping the thread clockwise, pick up one (1) or two (2) threads of material. (See Figure 36E.)

Pull the needle and thread up through the loop. (See Figure 37E.)

Insert the needle at the base of the loop, pulling the thread through to the wrong side. (See Figure 38E.)

NOTE: Using six (6) strands of thread, this stitch is ideal for forming cherries, grapes, or holly berries.

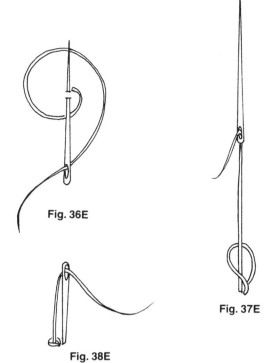

Fig. 36E

Fig. 37E

Fig. 38E

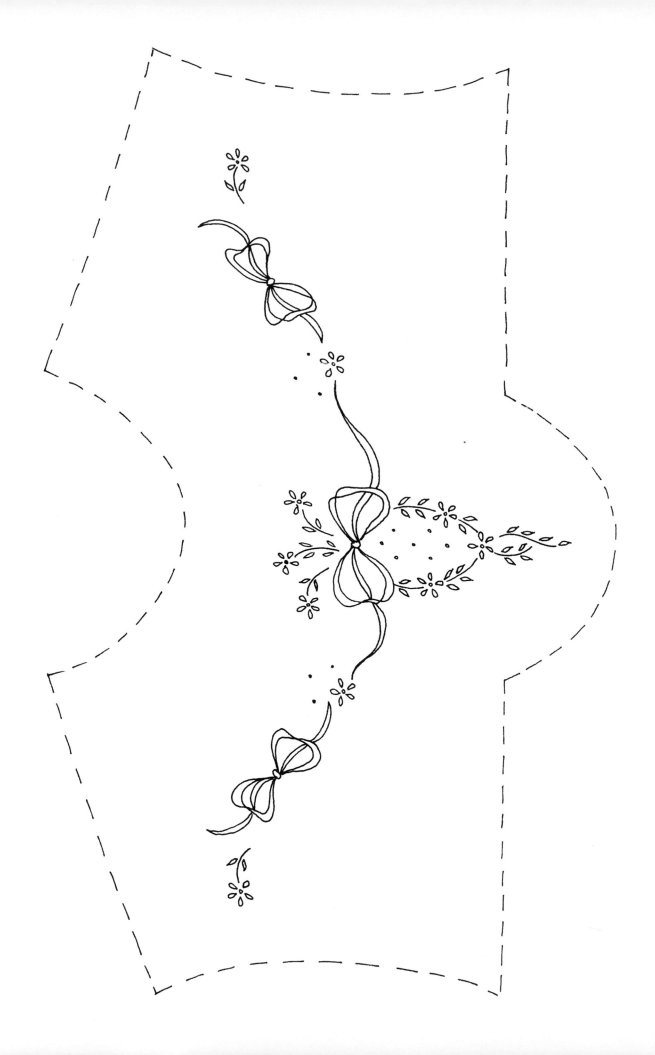

HEMSTITCH

Hemstitching creates a lovely insertion or a finish for a hem, producing an openwork effect. A material in which the threads can be withdrawn must be used; materials such as batiste, linen or lawn would be excellent. There are many kinds of hemstitching, but the simpler ones lend themselves more effectively to French handsewing.

Begin by drawing out an even number of threads (the number depending upon the width hemstitching will be.)

HALF HEMSTITCH

Working the stitches from left to right, with your needle take up the same number of threads that you have pulled out. (See Figure 39E.) Pull the needle and thread through to the right, side-pulling firmly, and make an additional stitch at the edge. (See Figure 40E.) The stitch that binds the thread should be almost invisible.

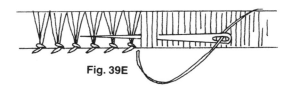

Fig. 39E

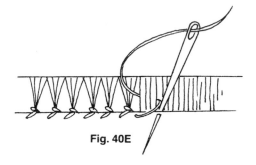

Fig. 40E

LADDER HEMSTITCH

Work the bottom edge of the drawn thread strip in the same manner as the Half Hemstitch. Turn work around so that the upper edge is now the lower edge and repeat. (See Figure 41E.) NOTE: Arrange the stitches so the same group of threads is bound together.

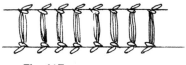

Fig. 41E

SERPENTINE OR ZIG-ZAG HEMSTITCH

Work the bottom edge of the drawn thread strip in the same manner as the Half Hemstitch.

After completion of the bottom row, work the upper row by dividing each group of threads evenly. (See Figure 42E.)
NOTE: If the group includes six (6) threads, divide it so three (3) threads are in one group and three (3) are in the next.

Fig. 42E

LAZY DAISY STITCH

The lazy daisy stitch is always worked on a single line or a narrow looped line. Slim petals and short narrow leaves are worked with it. Begin by bringing the needle and thread up at the inner end of the petal or leaf. Pass the needle down again through the same hole and bring the point out at the outer end of the petal of leaf. (See Figure 43E.) Before drawing the thread through, pass it under the point of the needle as for a buttonhole stitch. Draw the needle and thread through, holding the loop in place. Then, tack down the loop by passing the needle down again in the place from which it was just drawn (making a small stitch over the loop to hold it in place). (See Figure 44E.)

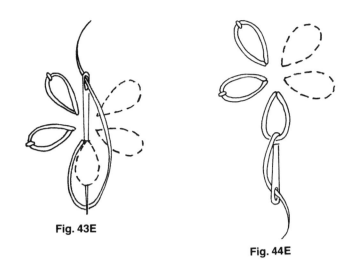

Fig. 43E

Fig. 44E

OUTLINE OR STEM STITCH

The outline stitch is frequently used by modern women to create the illusion of a stem. When using this stitch a conscious effort should be made to follow the line with small uniform stitches because the beauty of the stem is created in this way. (See Figure 45E.)

NOTE: The thread should always be below the needle and the stitch pulled toward the right. (See Figures 46E and 47E.)

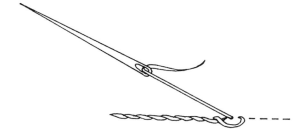

Fig. 45E

Fig. 46E

Fig. 47E

TATTED MEDALLION

AUTHENTIC STEM STITCH

This stitch must not be confused with the outline stitch. In white embroidery the latter should never be used. To make the stem stitch, first outline the line to be covered. Having done so, work over and over the outline stitches, with whipping stitches that are put in evenly and smoothly, that are close together, but never overlapping. These stitches should be made around the outline stitch and not through the material. (See Figure 48E.)

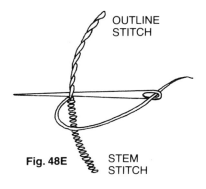

Fig. 48E

OUTLINE STITCH

STEM STITCH

RIGHT COLLAR

LEFT COLLAR

107

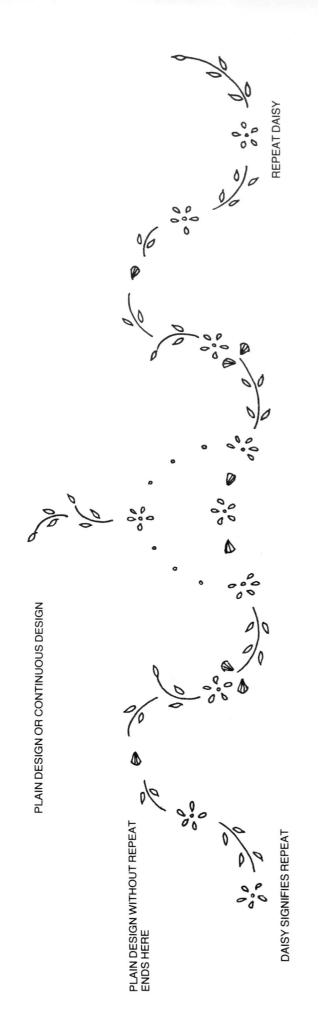

REPEAT DAISY

PLAIN DESIGN OR CONTINUOUS DESIGN

PLAIN DESIGN WITHOUT REPEAT
ENDS HERE

DAISY SIGNIFIES REPEAT

REPEAT DESIGN
CONNECTION

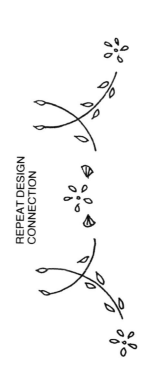

THE SNAIL TRAIL OR KNOTTED OUTLINE STITCH

This stitch seems very well suited to its name and is an effective form of decoration. It is made by combining a couching stitch with the outline stitch. For this reason, it is frequently called, by many embroiderers, a couched outline stitch.

It is done by bringing the thread up from the underside of the fabric, forming a loop with the thread, then inserting the needle into the material underneath the left side of the loop, and bringing the point of the needle up through the loop. The thread is drawn tightly to form a knot. The stitch should be repeated to form knots 1/4 inch apart.

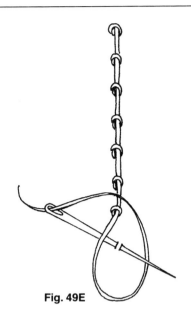

Fig. 49E

SATIN STITCH
FLOWER PETAL

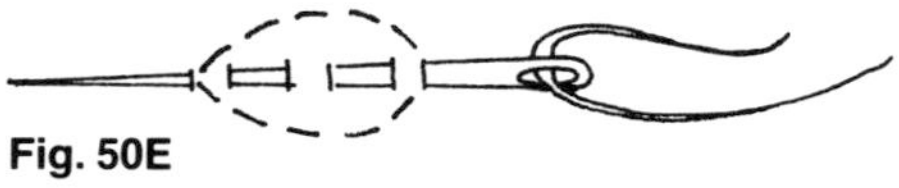

Fig. 50E

Fig. 51E

Fig. 52E

Fig. 53E

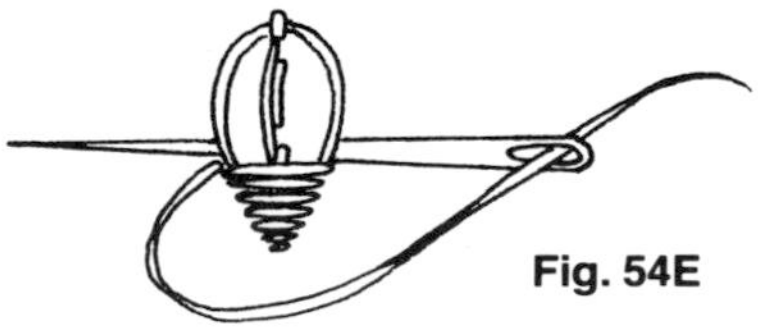

Fig. 54E

SATIN STITCH

I would like to show you the method I use to satin stitch the dainty leaf and flower petals that you see in most of my embroidery motifs. I use a size 12 needle and one (1) strand of fine embroidery thread.

FLOWER PETAL — Start at the top edge of the petal on the right side of the material and sew two running stitches to the base. (See Figure 50E.) NOTE: Do not knot thread; gently pull until the end of the thread is even with the top edge of the petal.

Insert needle at the top of the petal and bring needle and thread through the material and back to the base, making one (1) long stitch. (See Figure 51E.)

Complete the padding for the petal with a lazy daisy stitch. (See Figures 52E and 53E.) Satin stitch with very even stitches from the base to the top. (See Figure 54E.)

Take the needle and thread down to the wrong side of the fabric and run the needle under the threads to secure. (See Figure 55E.)

LEAF — Start at the top edge of the leaf on the right side of the material and sew two (2) running stitches to the base. (See Figure 56E.) NOTE: Do not knot thread; gently pull until the end of the thread is even with the top edge of the leaf.

Insert needle at the top of the leaf and bring needle and thread through the material and back to the base, making one (1) long stitch. (See Figure 57E.) Repeat. (See Figure 58E.)

Satin stitch with very even stitches from the base to the top. (See Figure 59E.)

NOTE: Each petal or leaf should be done separately and the thread clipped.

ROSE — Work Eyelet center first.

Outline the shape of the petal with tiny running stitches.

Fill the inside of the flower petal with padding stitches then satin stitch. (See Figure 60E.)

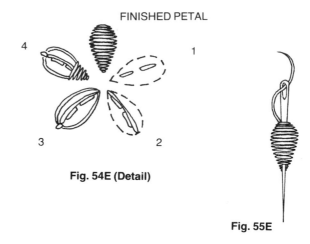

FINISHED PETAL

Fig. 54E (Detail)

Fig. 55E

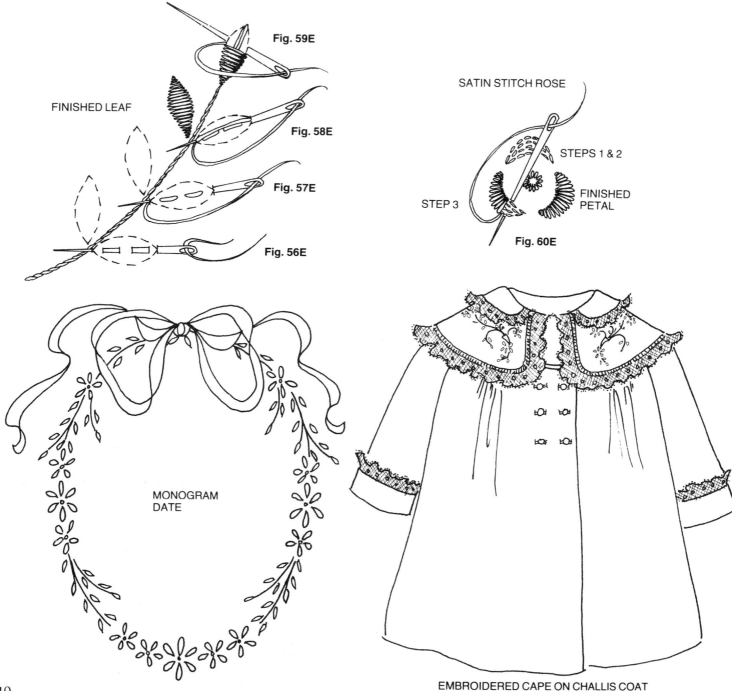

Fig. 59E

FINISHED LEAF

Fig. 58E

Fig. 57E

Fig. 56E

SATIN STITCH ROSE

STEPS 1 & 2

STEP 3

FINISHED PETAL

Fig. 60E

MONOGRAM
DATE

EMBROIDERED CAPE ON CHALLIS COAT

THESE DESIGNS FOLLOW ONE ANOTHER AROUND THE BANDS
IN THE SKIRT.

EMBROIDERY DESIGN FOR CAPE ON
CHALLIS COAT

EMBROIDERED PLACKET ON DAYGOWN

EMBROIDERY DESIGN FOR PLACKET ON DAYGOWN

BUTTONHOLING A PADDED SCALLOP

Start a scallop to be worked in buttonholing by running its inner and outer edges with stitches sufficiently small enough to retain the shape of the scallop. Fill between the edges with padding stitches, keeping them long on the right side and short on the wrong side, and have them swing with the curves of the scallop. Now begin to buttonhole. The work should be in a hoop, the outer edge of the scallop toward the worker. Fasten the thread with a few running stitches in the padded part, and bring the needle up through the outer edge at the extreme left. Pass the needle down on the inner edge at the extreme left and bring the point out on the outer edge to the right of the stitch first taken. Pass the loop of thread under the point and draw out the needle. All the stitches are made in this way, swinging them gradually, so that the needle is placed, for each stitch, exactly horizontal to the edges of the scallop at that point. (See Figure 61E.)

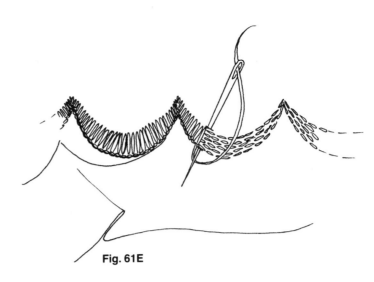

Fig. 61E

BUTTONHOLING A COUCHING SCALLOP

This method is used for small narrow scallops. Draw or trace the scallop design on the material and couch the outline of the scallops with six strands of embroidery thread. (See Couching Figure 63E.) Cover the couching with a buttonhole stitch, using one strand of embroidery thread. (See Figure 62E.)
NOTE: Material should not be cut away from scallop until the buttonholing is complete.

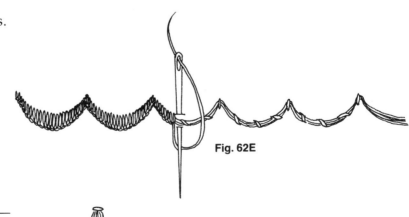

Fig. 62E

COUCHING

As shown by the illustration, couching consists of six (6) strands of thread laid smoothly together and secured in place by stitches brought from the back of the material and passed over the threads to the wrong side again.

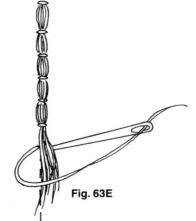

Fig. 63E

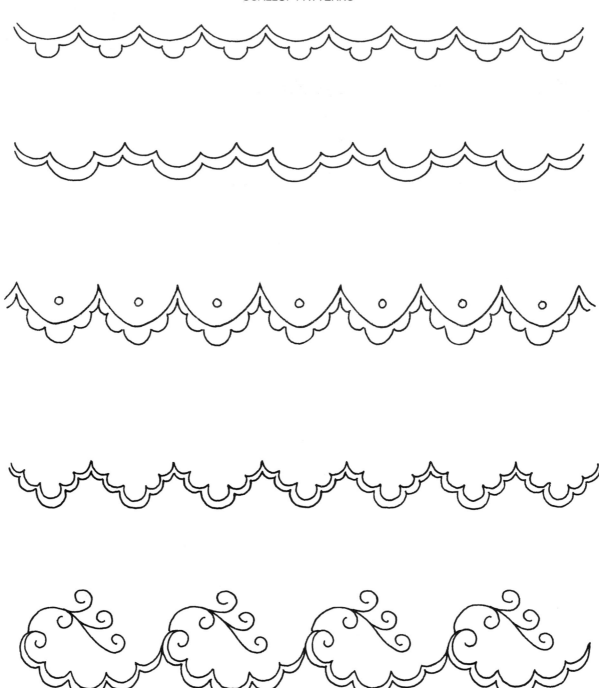

SEED STITCH

The Seed Stitch is another important stitch of French embroidery. It is actually nothing more than the "back stitch" of sewing, and is used as a filling-in stitch for leaves and petals that are too wide to permit the use of the raised satin stitch. (See Figure 64E.) Such leaves and petals usually have narrow, satin stitch edges and centers covered with seed stitch. Seed stitching is put in regular rows, sometimes wide apart and sometimes close together. The closer together the rows are, the prettier the effect will be. In very fine pieces of French embroidery, the seed stitches are about the size of a pin head and have a space the size of a pin head between them.

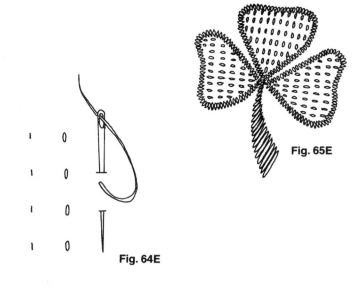

Fig. 65E

Fig. 64E

SHADOW WORK

Shadow work is done on very sheer fabrics such as organdy, batiste, and lawn. Bows, flowers, and leaves take on a pleasing effect when worked in this way. The beauty of shadow work depends on the stitches showing through strongly, so use as many strands of thread as you need (usually one (1) to four (4) strands) to achieve the look you want.
NOTE: For the motifs in this book, I prefer to use one (1) strand.

The stitches appear as two (2) rows of backstitching on the right side and as a crossed or close herringbone stitch on the wrong side. It is necessary to make small backstitches in order to form close crossed stitches.

Work the design on the right side of the material. (See Figure 66E.)

Bring the needle and thread up to the right upper edge of the design and make one (1) backstitch, slipping the needle under the material in a slanted position so that it emerges on the lower edge one (1) stitch to the left of the starting point. Proceed working as shown in Figure 67E.

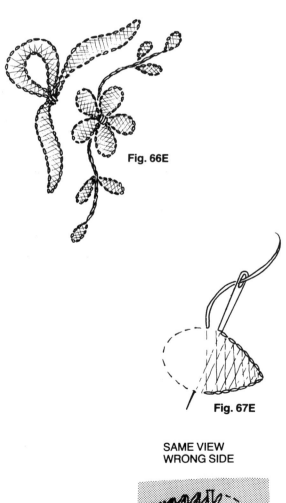

Fig. 66E

Fig. 67E

SAME VIEW
WRONG SIDE

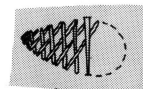

HOW INITIALS ARE WORKED

The illustration shows clearly the three steps in the working of the raised satin stitch for initial letters. (See Figure 68E.) The edges must be run first. This is an important step, for upon it depends much of the appearance of the edges and the smoothness of the outlines of the letter.

Whether satin stitch or stem stitch is used for a letter, begin by running the outline with small stitches that do not spoil the lines. Then fill between with padding stitches, making them close together in the center of the wide part of the letter, and spacing them more widely in the narrow part, so that the wide part, when the satin stitch is worked, is higher.

The satin stitch is worked in the usual method, but the stitches must curve with the letter, and this must be done carefully to keep the work smooth. In rounding the curve, each stitch must be a little closer to the preceding stitch on the inner edge than on the outer, and it is by this means that the curve is secured. Be sure that the edges are even.

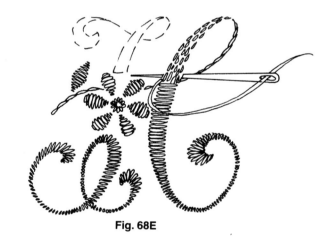

Fig. 68E

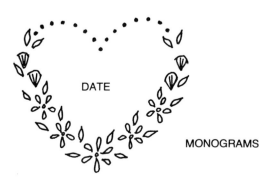

DATE

MONOGRAMS

MONOGRAM

116

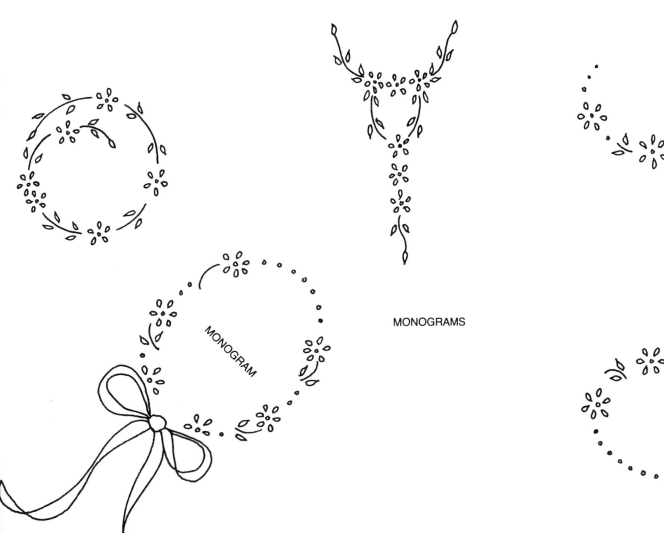

MONOGRAMS

MONOGRAM

DATE

Design for Christening Slip Skirt

A B C D E F G H
I J K L M N O P Q
R S T U V W X Y Z
0 1 2 3 4 5 6 7 8 9

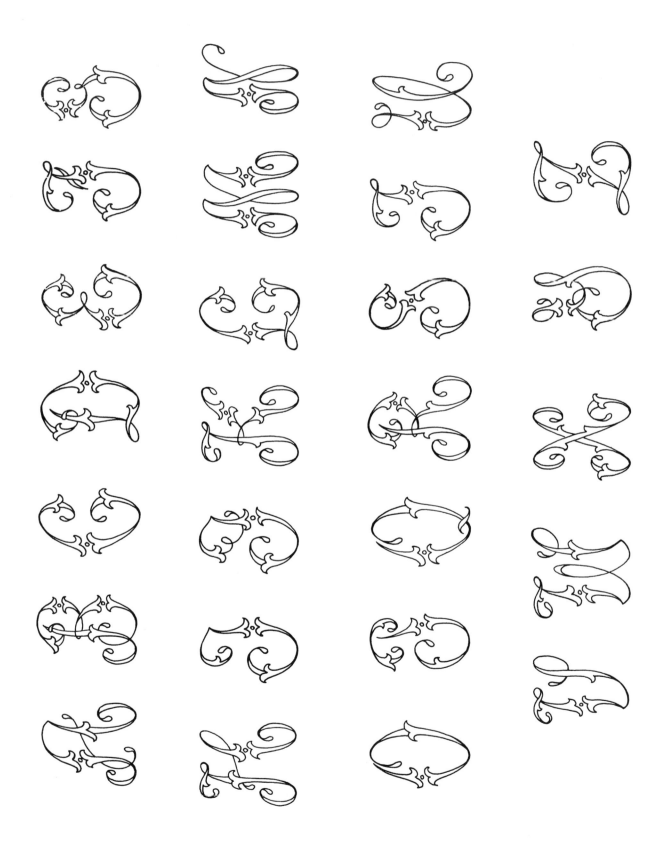

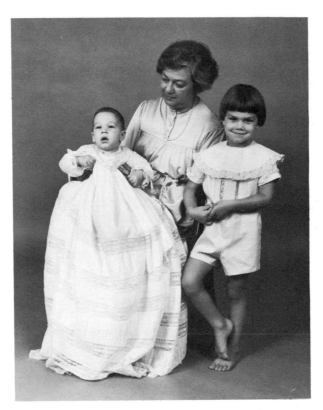

Sarah Howard Stone, who learned the art of French handsewing from her mother, is today nationally known as the Master of French Handsewing. Sarah, through her sewing classes, has instilled a love of handsewing in the hearts of hundreds of young women, thus insuring the survival of the art.

She has served on the faculty of the Embroiderers' Guild of America and The Valentine Assembly. Sarah travels throughout the United States conducting seminars and trunk shows for needlework guilds, specialty shops, and charitable organizations. She established the Mary Oliver McLemore Scholarship Fund, from proceeds of her fashion shows and from private donations, to aid deserving young women in furthering their college educations.

With this book, Sarah Howard Stone gives clear, concise written instructions in the art of French handsewing. This is a first! No more lost notes or forgotten instructions. Sarah is giving herself with this book, and everyone who has ever handsewn a delicate garment will be grateful. What Sarah cannot give is that which makes her a true artist — her creative genius. Because she has shared that with us through the years, we are grateful.

ACKNOWLEDGEMENTS

Photography .... Robertson Photography, Inc.
John L. Finklea, M.D.
Editing .... Marion Motley
Offset Lithography .... Walker Printing Company, Inc.
Montgomery, Alabama

A special thanks to The Landmarks Foundation,
Montgomery, Alabama, for allowing us to photograph
our subjects at the Ordeman Shaw House and
Cooper Cottage

MODELS:

Elizabeth Butler
Mary Virginia Butler
Virginia Moody Butler
Ann Smith Carothers
Allison Finklea
Tyler Finklea
Hunter Frazer
Margaret Frazer
Amanda Garrison
Corinne Graddick
Davis Benton Marshall
Rebecca Stone Marshall
Samuel Allen Marshall III
Kathryn Moore
Le Arden Rocheleau
Caroline Stone
Melissa Stone
Shea Sumners
Glenn Byron Sylvest Jr.
Ann Harris Webb
Clinton Lewis Wilson
Marguerite Zoghby